Arya Nair

Arya Nair, a 16-year-old Science student, was born in Thrissur but currently resides in the UAE with her parents. She began her educational journey at Smt. Vidyaben Gardi High School in Mulund, Mumbai, where she completed her primary schooling. Arya is now a dedicated Grade 11 student at Ryan International School, Sharjah. In addition to her creative pursuits, Arya also harbours aspirations to pursue medicine as her chosen profession.

Despite her rigorous study schedule, Arya's insomniac nature makes her a night owl, allowing her to burn the midnight oil while crafting compelling stories and poems. Her creative pursuits are not hindered by her academic commitments. With an ambivert personality, she thrives in outgoing and fun social interactions, but can just as easily immerse herself in her own world when chasing creative adventures.

This marks the second book in Arya's highly acclaimed series, 'Chronicles of the Sisterhood.' Her debut book, 'The Mystery of the Smiley Mask,' achieved bestseller status.

English Language
Shards in the Sky
(Novel)
 by
Arya Nair

Published in November 2023
by Decan Imprint Publishing Co.
Reg. Off: Sharjah Publishing City
Free Zone Sharjah, UAE.
Phone: 00971-551830334
Email : decanimprint@gmail.com

Cover Paintings & Illustrations
Arya Nair

Cover Design
Prasanth Mangad

Printed at
Printing Park, Tly.

08/23-24/Sl.No.08/250/18.6 NS.
ISBN 978-93-5973-726-3

Chronicles of the Sisterhood!

Shards in the Sky

Arya Nair

DECANIMPRINT

Dedicated to my Great Grandmom,
Smt. Saradamma. M.
(May her soul be at peace)

FORWARD

A wave of pride has swept through the hallways of Ryan International School Sharjah, and at the heart of this joyous ripple is Ms. Arya Nair. With her newly published book "Shards in the Sky" Arya has etched another chapter in the captivating 'Chronicles of the Sis -terhood series, setting a shining example for her peers.

As the Principal, it's moments like these that reaffirm my belief in our education system,our teaching staff, and the boundless potential of our students. Arya's journey is a shining example of where dedication and passion can lead.

I encourage every member of our school community to read and support Arya's work. Let's celebrate this moment and rally behind our young star. May her literary journey be filled with continued growth, inspiration, and grace, and may her words always find their rightful place among the stars.

With Pride,
Ms. Daizy Paul
Principal,
Ryan International School

Content

Chapter 1

The Enigmatic Beginning!

"Oh My God! Are you serious?"Elena sat perched on the edge of her couch, clutching her phone with eager anticipation as she listened to her sister, Erica, share some life-changing news. The sound of Erica's voice was a symphony of joy and excitement that travelled through the wires and right into Elena's heart. "Elena," Erica exclaimed, "You won't believe it!

John proposed to me and I said Yes! I'm getting married!Elena's eyes widened with delight, and a rush of emotions surged within her. "My sister is getting married, guys". Her girl gang or the Sisterhood as they called themselves, Isabella, Sophia, Amelia, and Olivia erupted in jubilation. Their Sisterhood was a tapestry of shared memories and experiences.

As Elena relayed the incredible news, the Sisterhood bounced with delight. Isabella, the hopeless romantic, swooned over the proposal details. Sophia, the pragmatic one, immediately began offering her organizational skills for wedding planning. Amelia,Isabella and Olivia, the life of the party trio, were already plotting unforgettable celebrations.

Elena was elated as her closest friends rejoiced in Erica's love story. In that flurry of phone calls, laughter, and jubilation, Elena felt a deep sense of gratitude for the bond of friendship that surrounded her. With her sister's wedding on the horizon, it was clear that their tight-knit group would embark on a journey filled with love, laughter, and unforgettable moments.

The news of Erica's engagement had ignited a spark of excitement that would light up their lives in the days and months to come. For the Sisterhood bound together by a deep bond forged through shared experiences and unwavering support, the journey ahead was more than just another escapade.

It was a voyage filled with challenges, personal growth, and above all the unbreakable ties of Sisterhood. In their previous adventure, the Sisterhood had been thrust into a harrowing ordeal where they came face to face with a deranged murderer. They had not only managed to unmask the killer but also played a pivotal role in ensuring that the killer was caught and put behind bars.

The experience had left an indelible mark on their bond, forging it into something unbreakable. However, their journey didn't end there. United by a sense of righteousness and an unwavering commitment to making the world a better place, the Sisterhood found that true justice hadn't been served. They soon delved into a quest to seek justice for a forgotten victim of bullying.

As they plunged into the complexities of the case, they uncovered a web of secrets, pain, and injustice that had long been hidden. With their unity growing stronger with every trial they faced, the members of the Sisterhood emerged not only as survivors but as a formidable team, a force to be reckoned with. The Sisterhood was not to be trifled with.

Their dogged determination to right the wrongs of the world made them an unstoppable collective. Their past adventures served as a testament to their unwavering commitment to making the world a better place, one act of justice at a time. Each girl brought to the table a unique set of strengths, skills, and talents that harmonized seamlessly, forming an unstoppable collective force.

Amelia, with her short, neatly cropped hair, was the brainiac among the Sisterhood of five remarkable girls. Her sharp intellect shone through her expressive eyes, hidden behind a stylish pair of rectangular glasses that seemed perfectly at home on her face. She was the group's intellectual anchor, always armed with a book in one hand and a penchant for solving complex problems.

Amelia's no-nonsense demeanour and unyielding determination were balanced by her warm heart and unwavering support for her sisters. In this Sisterhood of diverse talents and personalities, Amelia's brilliance was the North Star that guided them through the challenges of life. And her short hair symbolized the practicality that grounded their unique bond.

Olivia, the second member of the Sisterhood embodied a spirit that was both brave and bold, wrapped in an aura of unbridled adventure. Her long, tousled hair seemed to mirror her untamed enthusiasm for life. With a mischievous glint in her eyes, she fearlessly embraced every challenge that came her way. She was the one who guided them into thrilling adventures.

She led them on spontaneous road trips, scaled towering cliffs, and fearlessly pursued her passions. Her infectious courage was a constant source of inspiration, reminding the Sisterhood to live life to the fullest. In the vibrant fabric of the Sisterhood, Olivia's adventurous soul was the vivid thread that added a touch of exhilaration to their shared journey.

Sophia, the guarded and intelligent anchor of the Sisterhood, possessed an understated elegance that mirrored her composed demeanour. Her long, chestnut hair cascaded gracefully down her back, framing a face adorned with glasses that accentuated her studious nature. She was the voice of reason in the group, carefully weighing every decision and mapping out thoughtful plans.

Sophia's remarkable intelligence was matched only by her kindness, making her the reliable source of wisdom and a pillar of support for her sisters. In the Sisterhood's dynamic blend of personalities, Sophia's cautious approach and keen intellect formed a steadfast foundation, guiding them through the storms of life with grace and poise.

Isabella, the fiercely loyal guardian of the Sisterhood had an exterior as tough as a coconut, shielding a heart of pure, unconditional love for her sisters. Her long, flowing hair, often wild and free, was a reflection of her untamed spirit. Isabella was always ready to stand up and fiercely defend her sisters, regardless of the challenges that came their way.

She had an unyielding determination, much like the strength it took to crack open a coconut. She would never back down from a fight when it came to protecting her chosen family. Isabella's unwavering devotion was the unbreakable bond that fortified the Sisterhood's connection, making her a formidable force to be reckoned with and a true pillar of strength for all.

Elena, the hopeless romantic, often wore her heart on her sleeve, making her endearingly vulnerable. Her hair flowing in loose waves framed her expressive face, reflecting her ever-changing emotions. A tendency to dive headfirst into love's depths occasionally led her into questionable choices. But her unwavering belief in the power of love was a guiding light for the group.

But when the going got tough, Elena's innate bravery shone through. She would fearlessly confront challenges, drawing from her heart's deepest reserves of courage. In the Sisterhood's mosaic of personalities, Elena's romantic spirit added a touch of whimsy and warmth, reminding all to cherish the beauty in life's most tender moments while bravely facing whatever obstacles lay ahead.

The Sisterhood had weathered storms together. And now, they were ready to reap the rewards of their hard-won successes. Their academic pursuits had been relentless demanding a level of dedication that had often tested their limits. But today, those burdens were laid to rest. And they could finally savour the sweet freedom of a well-deserved vacation.

Elena radiated an infectious excitement. Her eyes sparkled with an extra layer of brilliance. Her laughter was infused with newfound joy, and there was an unmistakable spring in her step. Erica, Elena's beloved sister was soon to embark on a life-altering journey of her own, a journey that involved a commitment so profound that it warranted a celebration unlike any other.

Erica was getting married, and the thought of sharing in this monumental moment filled Elena's heart with immeasurable delight. As the girls sat together in Elena's cosy living room, their minds began to buzz with possibilities. They imagined the upcoming festivities, the vibrant colours, the enchanting music, and the fragrant flowers that would adorn the wedding venue.

They speculated about the delectable dishes that would grace the banquet table, the dances that would swirl with graceful exuberance, and the sheer euphoria of it all. They would not merely be spectators at this joyous event. No, Elena's parents had extended a heartfelt invitation, urging the Sisterhood to be active participants in the celebrations.

They wanted them to be more than just witnesses. They wanted them to be a vital part of the mosaic of this significant event. The invitation underscored the importance of these bonds in Elena's life and their collective significance. To Elena and her friends, it was a gesture of love and inclusion, a testament to the idea that in their hearts, the bonds of friendship were as treasured as those of blood.

Erica's wedding was set amidst the vivid landscapes of India.

The prospect of travelling to a land steeped in history, culture, and tradition filled them with a sense of wonder and curiosity. India was not merely a destination; it was a magical realm where ancient customs danced with contemporary celebrations, creating a symphony of colours, sounds, and emotions.

This event, they knew, had the potential to forge priceless memories that would be etched into their hearts for a lifetime. It was an opportunity to revel in a unique and thrilling adventure together, to explore a rich and diverse culture, and to witness the divine beauty of a love that transcended boundaries. They were absolutely delighted about the forthcoming celebrations.

From the vibrant pre-wedding rituals that would herald the impending union to the solemnity of the wedding ceremony itself, the trip promised a kaleidoscope of experiences. It was an extraordinary opportunity to not only connect with Indian culture and traditions, but also to strengthen the already unbreakable bond that held the Sisterhood together.

The five friends, Elena, Isabella, Sophia, Amelia, and Olivia gathered excitedly at Elena's comfy home in Dubai. They were about to embark on a thrilling adventure, starting with a journey to Dubai Airport to catch their Emirates flight to Mumbai. Elena's house buzzed with the excitement of their upcoming trip as they made their final preparations.

Their luggage, neatly packed and filled with anticipation stood in a corner of Elena's living room. Sophia, the organized one, meticulously checked their passports and travel documents to ensure a smooth journey. Amelia and Olivia, the adventurous duo, couldn't contain their excitement, talking animatedly about all the places they planned to visit in Mumbai.

Sophia double-checked everything to ensure they had everything they needed for the trip. With laughter and chatter filling the air, they piled into a waiting taxi bound for Dubai Airport. As the city of Sharjah faded into the distance, their hearts were filled with the promise of new experiences, unforgettable memories, and the excitement of the adventure that lay ahead.

Chapter 2

Voyage to the Unknown!

After a short yet exhilarating journey from Dubai on Emirates Airlines, the five friends finally touched down in India. As they stepped off the plane and into the bustling Chhatrapati Shivaji Maharaj International Airport, the sensory overload was immediate; a symphony of scents, sounds, and colours that wrapped them in a warm, exotic embrace.

This was more than a vacation. It was a cultural odyssey, a chance to immerse themselves in a world that was both familiar and foreign. As they navigated the vibrant streets of Mumbai, their senses were continuously tantalized. The aroma of street food filled the air. And the lively chatter of locals mixed with the honking of rickshaws and the occasional burst of traditional music.

The Sisterhood were open to the spontaneity of the city, ready to embrace every new experience and adventure that awaited them. Excitement enveloped them like a cocoon. In the heart of India, amidst the vibrant embroidery of cultures and traditions, the Sisterhood was set to create unforgettable memories that would forever bind them in the warm embrace of friendship and discovery.

Venturing through bustling markets, they savoured aromatic spices, and marvelled at the hustle and bustle of this ancient city. The City of Mumbai with its juxtaposition of old-world charm and modern energy served as the backdrop for their adventure. From exploring historical landmarks to savouring delectable street food, they embraced the beauty of India's diversity.

Their laughter echoed through crowded streets of Mumbai, a captivating blend of historic colonial architecture and towering

skyscrapers, where the Arabian Sea met a cityscape teeming with life.

Elena's privileged background had its perks. As they arrived at the iconic Taj Mahal Hotel, their accommodations exceeded all expectations. The grandeur of the Queen Suite left the girls awestruck. The room was a masterpiece of opulence, adorned with intricate tapestries and ornate furnishings that seemed to have been plucked from the pages of a fairy tale.

As they stepped into the lavish suite, their collective gasps of amazement echoed through the room. The tapestries told stories of a bygone era, depicting scenes of royalty and grandeur. The ornate chandeliers cast a warm, golden glow over the room, adding to the enchantment. Soft, plush furnishings beckoned them to relax and soak in the luxury that surrounded them.

Wide-eyed with wonder, they couldn't help but feel like royalty themselves. In this magnificent setting, they knew that their adventure in India was about to become an even more extraordinary and unforgettable experience. Sophia, the organizer of the group had left no stone unturned in meticulously planning this trip to India. She had judiciously orchestrated every single detail.

Recognizing the significance of the occasion for Elena's family, and the upcoming wedding, Amelia undertook extensive research on Indian customs and traditions.Her dedication was a testament to the utmost respect they had for the local culture. Amelia taught them the significance of traditional Indian attire as well as familiarized them with the traditional wedding rituals.

Elena, the fashionista of the group and the bride's sister couldn't contain her excitement any longer. With a gleeful twinkle in her eye, she unveiled a stunning array of traditional Indian attire. She had chosen the outfits meticulously for every girl in the Sisterhood. The room seemed to come alive with a burst of colours and exquisite fabrics that spilled across the bed, captivating the senses.

As Elena lifted each sari, her enthusiasm was infectious. She envisioned all of them donning these vibrant, gracefully-flowing saris, each piece a living canvas that would beautifully showcase the kaleidoscope of colors and cultures of India. The Sisterhood were enthusiastic about the prospect of embracing Indian traditions and experiencing their rich diversity.

With every garment, she explained the significance of the design, the symbolism behind the colours, and the elegance of the patterns. The Sisterhood couldn't help but be swept up in Elena's infectious passion. They were astounded by Elena's flair for traditional fashion. They marvelled at the intricacies of the garments and the artistry that had gone into their creation.

As they held their respective saris, they knew that they were not just beautiful pieces of clothing but a gateway to a deeper understanding of India's rich heritage. Amelia, the brainiac and the avid reader of the group had become a veritable fountain of knowledge in the weeks leading up to their journey to India. She devoured everything related to India and its culture.

Her excitement and enthusiasm for all things related to Indian history and culture were contagious, often leading her to explain everything excitedly and loudly to the amusement of the Sisterhood. As they sat together, whether in their lavish hotel suite or during their explorations of Mumbai, Amelia's animated explanations about India's rich heritage filled the air.

She regaled them with stories of ancient dynasties, the significance of colourful festivals, the deep sense of spirituality that infused every aspect of Indian life. She elaborated on the various festivals of India and their historical significance. Her eyes sparkled with admiration for the traditions they were about to witness, and her deep respect for the culture resonated with the group.

Despite the occasional chuckles and good-natured teasing about her enthusiastic explanations, the Sisterhood valued Amelia's boundless curiosity and her eagerness to share her knowledge with the group. Amelia's excitement was like a torch illuminating the path they were all eager to explore, guiding them with its infectious energy.

Olivia and Isabella, the ever brave and strong-willed duo of the group carried an air of caution amidst their shared excitement for the adventure. While they were eager to dive headfirst into every experience that India had to offer, they couldn't help but wear the cloak of vigilance. Their protective instincts and keen awareness of potential dangers made them the voice of reason in the group.

Olivia and Isabella gently warned the Sisterhood not to become complacent. Their experiences from past adventures had honed their ability to assess situations and take calculated risks, and they wanted their friends to do the same. It wasn't about stifling their enthusiasm, but rather ensuring that they would venture forth with open hearts and open eyes.

Elena moved gracefully through the suite, her radiant smile

illuminating every corner. Her family had gone above and beyond in their preparations for the arrival of her friends. Elena couldn't contain her excitement, eager for her dear friends to immerse themselves in the beauty of India; the delectable cuisine, the intricate artistry, and the boundless hospitality of her homeland.

But what filled her heart with the greatest joy was the realization that her friends were now an integral part of her family's most revered celebration. Their presence added an extra layer of warmth and love to the upcoming wedding, turning it into a true union of hearts and cultures. Elena's smile was a reflection of the deep sense of unity and camaraderie that defined their Sisterhood.

The adventurous spirits of the Sisterhood were practically bursting with eagerness to explore the bustling streets of Mumbai. They longed to lose themselves in the labyrinthine bazaars, relish the myriad flavours of street food, and capture the vibrant scenes with their cameras. Each step they took felt like a journey into the heart of India's rich culture and history.

Amidst the cacophony of sounds and the kaleidoscope of colours, they had an inkling that India held countless secrets waiting to be uncovered. Olivia's adventurous soul burned brightly, ready to dive into uncharted territories, while Isabella's protective instincts stood guard, ensuring they explored with caution. Their collective enthusiasm knew no bounds.

One sunny afternoon, amidst the joyful chaos of wedding preparations, Elena gathered her friends in the Taj courtyard, where a fragrant breeze carried hints of jasmine and incense. She stood before them, a radiant smile gracing her features. She cleared her throat to gain their attention. Her parents, Mr. & Mrs. Ramirez stood beside her.

Elena's gesture led the way to an elderly couple sitting together, wrapped in a spirited conversation. She introduced them warmly, saying, "And these are my grandparents, Abuelos and Abuela. They are the heart and soul of our family, the keepers of our traditions and stories."

The girls approached the elderly couple, whose eyes twinkled with wisdom and love.

Abuelos, his voice carrying the weight of years of experience, spoke with a warm smile. "Elena speaks so highly of her friends," he said, "It's a pleasure to finally meet you. Your presence at Erica's wedding is an honour for us. Please enjoy the wedding festivities. May they create precious souvenirs for all of you." His words echoed within them, caressing their hearts with love.

Abuela simply extended her arms to embrace each of the girls in a warm and affectionate hug. "Indeed," she added with a warm smile, "Our family is blessed to have Elena's friends here to share in this special time." Her gentle words filled the air with a sense of inclusion and love, making the girls feel welcome in Elena's close-knit family.

As the introductions continued, Elena led her friends through the lively gathering, illuminating various family members and their pivotal roles in the wedding preparations. The girls met a delightful array of cousins, aunts, and uncles, each immersed in their tasks to ensure every detail was perfect. Among them were Miguel, Juan, and Carolina, Elena's spirited cousins.

The atmosphere buzzed with excitement as they connected with Elena's family and cousins. Miguel, a young man with a perpetual twinkle in his eye and an infectious enthusiasm, spoke up, "Hello, Amelia, Olivia, Isabella, and Sophia! We're thrilled to have you here. Let's make this wedding an unforgettable experience". Juan, equally enthusiastic and brimming with energy, chimed in.

"Absolutely! Our motto is 'Work hard, play harder.' Get ready for a whirlwind of festivities and celebrations". Carolina, the vivacious cousin with a flair for creativity, added with a wink, "Get ready to transform into Bollywood stars! We'll teach you dance moves so sizzling, even the candles will blush, and the moon will wish it could join our dance party in the sky!"

Christopher, the resident comic, was Mr. Ronald's son, and Erica's childhood friend. He had a knack for cracking jokes that could make even the most serious moments burst into peals of laughter. His infectious sense of humour had the entire gathering in stitches. Chris, always ready with a witty remark, couldn't resist cracking a joke.

With a mischievous grin, he quipped, "Why did the tomato turn red? Because it saw the salad dressing!" His playful humour filled the air, eliciting laughter from everyone around and adding a delightful touch of light-heartedness to the festivities. Chris, sensing the opportunity for another laugh, chimed in, "Why don't skeletons fight each other? Because they don't have the guts!"

His clever wordplay earned him another round of hearty laughter from the crowd, making him the life of the pre-engagement celebration. Sophia, known for her stern and pragmatic demeanour, surprised everyone by laughing the loudest at Chris' jokes. Her newfound appreciation for his humour didn't go unnoticed by the others.

Olivia, with a teasing grin, chimed in, "His jokes aren't that funny, you know." Sophia responded crossly, saying, "I find them funny. What's your problem?". Amidst all the laughter and enjoyment, the pre-engagement function approached. It was an informal gathering, bringing together the extended families and intimate circle of friends from both the bride and groom's side.

As the girls changed into their traditional Indian attire, the room became a melody of laughter and excitement. They huddled together, helping each other with the intricacies of draping a sari or fastening a kurta. In this shared experience of embracing a new culture, bonds between them grew stronger with every knot tied and pleat folded.

The pre-engagement function was a vibrant and joyous occasion, a harmonious blend of traditions and the warmth of new connections. Held in a beautifully decorated venue at the Taj, the gathering was an opportunity for John and Erica's extended families and close friends to come together and begin building the bonds that would unite them in the journey ahead.

As the evening sun dipped below the horizon, the atmosphere was filled with anticipation and excitement. Traditional Indian music played softly in the background, setting the tone for the festivities. Colourful decorations adorned the venue, with marigold garlands and twinkling fairy lights creating an enchanting ambiance.

Elena looked resplendent in a shimmering golden lehenga adorned with intricate sequins and beads, radiating elegance and style. Isabella's Anarkali suit was a burst of vibrant reds and pinks, with delicate embroidery, making her a vision of grace and charm. Sophia wore a graceful saree in shades of royal blue and silver, with a timeless elegance that showcased her respect for tradition.

Amelia's salwar kameez in a rich shade of emerald green, featured intricate patterns and mirror work, reflecting her love for cultural exploration. Olivia's fusion ensemble combined a chic kurta with lively prints and comfortable palazzo pants, capturing her adventurous spirit and lively personality. Guests, dressed in their finest attire, mingled and exchanged warm greetings.

The air was perfumed with the enticing aroma of Indian delicacies and sweets being prepared in the kitchen. Tables were adorned with a mouth-watering spread of flavourful and scrumptious chaats, savoury and crunchy samosas, crisp and spicy pakoras, and delectable sweets, inviting everyone to relish the flavours of India.

Erica donned an exquisite Indian lehenga choli in shades of deep maroon and gold, with intricate embroidery and a flowing dupatta. A beautiful Polki necklace with intricate designs and precious gemstones adorned her neck accentuating her elegance. She completed the attire with traditional Juttis, intricately embellished with golden threadwork and sparkling crystals.

John looked dashing in a classic Indian sherwani, a tailored masterpiece in rich royal blue and gold, adorned with intricate embellishments. His turban was a masterpiece of rich royal blue fabric adorned with intricate golden patterns. John completed his traditional look with intricately designed Mojdis with detailed embroidery and exquisite craftsmanship.

John and Erica, the undeniable focal point of the evening glided gracefully through the gathering, their smiles radiant as they orchestrated introductions between family members and friends. Amidst the lively atmosphere, laughter cascaded like a soothing melody. Animated conversations flowed as freely as the celebratory drinks. Stories intertwined, bridging gaps of culture and tradition.

Sophia's keen eyes though detected an imperceptible shadow, someone staring at Erica from a distance throughout the function. Amidst the joyful festivities, Sophia, perceptive as ever, caught a fleeting glimpse of a crack in Erica's facade of happiness. Yet, she chose to let it pass, attributing it to the stress that often accompanies such significant celebrations.

The countdown to the engagement ceremony was a crescendo of exhilaration, each moment a precious note in the melody of excitement. It was an upsurge of emotions, a kaleidoscope of butterflies in the stomach, and the perceptible thrum of hearts in synchrony. As the minutes dwindled, the atmosphere was pregnant with a sense of impending joy.

Laughter and chatter filled the air, forming a harmonious prelude to the grand celebration. The seconds turned to whispers of possibility, and the final countdown was a panorama of shared smiles and held breaths. It was a mosaic of dreams and aspirations that would soon come to life as two hearts united in the sacred promise of love and commitment.

Isabella was a vision of royal sophistication in her dazzling lehenga choli. The royal blue skirt was a canvas of intricate mirror work, reflecting a myriad of dazzling patterns. Her silver choli shimmered like moonlight perfected by a matching dupatta. Her attire was a masterpiece of craftsmanship, a dazzling, timeless ensemble.

Isabella adorned a stunning silver necklace encrusted with radiant diamonds, complemented by exquisite chandelier earrings. She put on intricately designed diamond bracelets. She wore ornate silver anklets that added a melodious jingle to her every step. Isabella's ensemble was perfectly complemented by her bejeweled silver Juttis.

Sophia chose a vibrant Anarkali suit with maroon and gold hues that echoed the hues of a setting sun, while the intricate floral patterns seemed to bloom with every step she took. The flowing silhouette of the Anarkali suit added an elegant grace to her movements, and the delicate embroidery told stories of tradition and artistry.

Sophia adorned herself with a stunning gold and emerald necklace perfected by ornate gold earrings, studded with emeralds. A matching gold bracelet adorned her wrist, while delicate anklets whispered with every step she took. Traditional juttis, embellished with intricate gold embroidery completed her look with a touch of majestic elegance.

Olivia's fusion ensemble was a delightful blend of contemporary chic and cultural fascination. Her kurta was a canvas of bold, abstract designs that appeared to leap off the fabric with avant-garde flair. The kurta's deep emerald green and rich ruby red hues created a striking contrast that was softened by intricate floral motifs. She elegantly paired it with comfortable palazzo pants.

Olivia's jewelry included a statement necklace adorned with emerald and ruby gemstones and matching Jhumka earrings. Her matchless bracelet was a mosaic of floral patterns. Her anklets were crafted with fine, silvery chains dangling with ornate charms. She completed her fusion look with comfortable and stylish embroidered mojdis.

Amelia embraced opulence in her exquisite lehenga, a striking blend of coral and silver. The skirt was adorned with delicate sequins that shimmered like a constellation of stars. Her silver choli, intricately patterned with traditional motifs, and a matching dupatta gracefully draped over her shoulders perfectly complemented the glittering skirt.

She wore a coral and silver necklace adorned with glistening gemstones. Her earrings reflected the same coral and silver hues. On her wrists, Amelia donned an exquisite bracelet featuring delicate silverwork. Her anklets featured intricate silver patterns that glistened under the light. Completing her look were coral and silver shoes, intricately designed to match her attire.

Elena, the epitome of grace, was adorned in an emerald green saree, intricately embroidered with golden threads that seemed to tell the tale of ancient forests. The fabric flowed like a tranquil river, each drape capturing the essence of tradition and the richness of her heritage. A matching golden blouse accentuated the regal elegance of her attire.

Her necklace featured an intricate tree of life design, adorned with emerald and golden accents. Her golden chandelier earrings were each adorned with a single emerald teardrop. She donned a set of golden bangles engraved with nature-inspired motifs. The golden anklets she wore featured tiny charms complemented by a pair of traditional juttis, hand-embroidered with golden and green threads.

Erica's dress was a masterpiece of sartorial artistry, a celestial gown that seemed to have been plucked from the realms of dreams. The fabric, a luminous blend of ivory and silver, flowed like moonlight on water, draping her in an ethereal aura. The intricate embroidery was a constellation of delicate stars, scattered across the bodice and trailing like comet tails down the flowing skirt.

A tiara adorned with glistening gemstones crowned her head. A magnificent choker encrusted with glistening diamonds and pearls paired with matching earrings sparkled like stars. Her ornate bangles and matching anklets with golden designs wove stories of tradition and love. Together with a pair of silver heels embellished with glimmering crystals, Erica transformed into a true Goddess.

Erica was a vision of unparalleled beauty. Her radiance surpassed even the brilliance of her attire and jewellery. "Erica, you're an absolute vision," Elena breathed in awe, her gaze fixed on her sister's ethereal beauty. Amelia, standing beside Elena, nodded in agreement, lost for words as they beheld Erica's transformation into a celestial being.

Today, Erica was not just beautiful; she was a living magnum opus, an artwork of grace and elegance woven into the fabric of this unforgettable moment. Elena's eyes glistened with unspoken emotions, the tears that welled up mirroring the deep love and happiness shared among the friends and sisters, encapsulating the essence of their lifelong bond.

Erica's blush deepened, painting her cheeks with a hue as delicate as the petals of a rose. "Thank you, my wonderful friends," she replied, her voice a melody of sincerity and affection. "I couldn't have dreamed of better bridesmaids and companions. Your presence here adds an indescribable sense of significance to this day." Her words were like a fragrant bouquet of appreciation.

Elena, Olivia, Amelia, Isabella, and Sophia formed a shield of unwavering support, ushering Erica into the ceremony hall. In the hushed ambiance, John stood, his gaze locked on Erica's luminous presence, as if time itself had paused to savour the enchanting sight. This moment marked the zenith of a love story that had blossomed like a secret garden since their earliest days.

John had harboured his feelings for Erica in the sacred vaults of his heart, never daring to imagine that they could bloom into reality. It took the gentle persuasion of his friends and a courageous leap of faith to finally utter the life-altering words. And now, in this surreal moment, the universe had conspired to grant his wish, making this day an embodiment of unexpected dreams and enduring love.

The engagement ceremony beckoned casting a spell of enchantment over the room. Bathed in the soft, ethereal glow of candlelight and surrounded by a fragrant garden of blossoms, the ambiance exuded an otherworldly romance. In the midst of their beloved friends and treasured family, Erica and John stood as if in a dream, ready to seal their love in the most remarkable way.

The engagement rings were exquisite symbols of love and commitment, each unique in its design. Erica's ring featured a dazzling, brilliant-cut diamond, set in a delicate band of platinum. The diamond sparkled with a brilliance that mirrored the radiance of her smile. John's ring was a band of white gold, intricately engraved with a pattern that symbolized their intertwined lives.

As they exchanged these symbols of their commitment, their families and friends' hearts swelled with joy and hope for the beautiful journey ahead. Amidst the celebrations and festivities, Sophia's perceptive instincts caught a glimpse of an enigmatic presence; a solitary figure whose gaze remained fixated on Erica. When she gazed once more, the figure had vanished into thin air.

While Erica's visage was a picture of unbridled happiness, her eyes betrayed a different narrative. To most, they sparkled with the brilliance of joy. Amidst the celebrations, Sophia sensed an underlying unease, like a haunting melody amidst the cheerful tunes. As the night unfurled, she made a silent promise to unravel the truth hidden behind the cryptic emotions in Erica's gaze.

As the days danced into nights, the wedding preparations ignited into a frenzy of creativity and dedication, akin to a symphony reaching its crescendo. The air seemed charged with the very essence of magic, as every facet of the celebration received meticulous attention. The venue transformed into a realm of enchantment, where dreams took shape and visions became reality.

One evening, in the midst of the grand festivities, the group of friends found solace in Erica's room, seeking a brief respite from the bustling preparations. It was during this quiet pause that Sophia's perceptive gaze fell upon Erica. Amidst the laughter and revelry that had surrounded Erica like a vibrant cloak, she sat on the edge of the bed, a portrait of melancholy.

Concern etched across her features; Sophia approached Erica. "Hey, Erica," she began. "Is there something you'd like to share? We're here for you." Sophia's words hung in the air. Erica's fingers moved with a swiftness born of practice, brushing away the glistening evidence of her tears. Her attempt to wear a brave mask was valiant, though her fragile voice betrayed her true emotions.

"Oh, Sophia," she replied softly. "It's just... I got a bit overwhelmed thinking about the significance of this wedding for my family and me." Sophia couldn't shake the feeling that there was more to the situation beneath the surface. Her instincts, finetuned by years of observation whispered that Erica's explanation might be just the surface of a deeper, unspoken truth.

However, respecting her need for privacy, she chose not to push further. Instead, she offered a reassuring smile. "I'm here whenever you're ready to share." "Thank you, Sophia," she whispered, her voice carrying the weight of unspoken emotions. "Anytime, Erica," Sophia replied. "We're here for you, always." Sophia's concern for Erica's unspoken sorrow led her to share this with the Sisterhood.

In a secluded room, away from the jubilant festivities, Sophia gathered the rest of the Sisterhood. She began by recounting the moments she had observed during the pre-engagement function; the shadowy figure gazing at Erica, the solitary figure at the engagement ceremony, and the emotional conversation with Erica. The Sisterhood realized that Erica was carrying a hidden burden.

Elena couldn't contain her worry any longer. "I've noticed," she confessed with a heavy heart, "That Erica has been shouldering an immense amount of pressure to ensure everything is perfect. But I didn't realize it was taking such a toll on her." The Sisterhood realized that amidst the wedding preparations, the weight of expectations had been quietly chipping away at Erica's well-being.

"Perhaps," Amelia suggested with a thoughtful air, "We can find a subtle way to unravel what's troubling Erica, all the while ensuring we don't burden her further. Amelia's suggestion garnered unanimous agreement. As the days of jubilation flowed on like a river, the Sisterhood kept a vigilant watch over Erica. Their hearts brimmed with a fierce determination to be her pillars of strength.

Yet, they couldn't disregard the whispering tendrils of doubt that suggested something was awry. Their watchful eyes noted subtle shifts in Erica's demeanour. Despite her efforts to maintain a facade of composure, her body language betrayed her struggle. Tension coiled within her, manifesting in the guarded posture of her shoulders, like a fortress wall protecting her vulnerability.

Her arms crossed protectively over her chest, as if to shield herself from the world's probing gaze. Though she valiantly tried to wear a smile and engage in conversation, there hung a poignant detachment. And her enthusiasm felt like a fragile façade, held together by sheer determination. It was as if her heart was a distant star, its light visible but untouchable.

There were occasions when Erica would subtly retreat from the centre of the group and slip into the background. Like fleeting shadows cast by a hidden moon, the Sisterhood couldn't help but catch occasional glimpses of sadness and fleeting expressions of sorrow that danced across her features. The Sisterhood were determined to unveil the hidden truth that burdened Erica's heart.

Unbeknownst to them, their quest for truth would prove to be an earthquake in their lives, a seismic event that would shake them to their very core. Their entire lives would be turned upside down. It was a chapter that promised not only revelations, but also challenges that would push them to their limits, a journey through an unknown, uncharted emotional terrain!

Chapter 3

The Mystery Deepens!

The room bathed in the morning sun, its golden tendrils gently caressing the space where Erica and her companions had made their home during the joyous wedding celebrations. This day had been etched into their hearts with eager anticipation; the day of Erica's wedding. An electric current of elation and delightful joy charged the air.

The Sisterhood readied themselves to witness Erica resplendent in her bridal regalia embark on a journey of love. Yet, in the midst of this serene morning, the tranquillity was shattered by a scream. A heart-wrenching scream cut through the room like a dagger resonating in the depths of every soul. It was Elena, Erica's younger sister, who had let out this anguished howl.

It was a cry of despair that seemed to rend the very fabric of the universe. The Sisterhood still ensconced in their sleepwear were jolted from their peaceful slumber. Their hearts raced with fear and confusion. They instinctively bolted upright in their beds; their eyes wide with alarm. The room was now cloaked in a shroud of uncertainty. They knew that something had gone terribly wrong.

With urgency coursing through their veins, they sprinted to Elena's room. Panic clung to them as they entered the room, their eyes locking onto Elena's trembling form. Tears flowed down her face like a river of sorrow. In her quivering hand, she clutched a crumpled letter, its contents enveloped in mystery. Their hearts pounded in their chests as they gathered around Elena.

"What's happened, Elena?", Sophia's voice quivered with genuine concern as she reached out to comfort her distraught friend. "What's wrong?" Elena, her sobs making it difficult to speak, managed to thrust the letter into Sophia's trembling hands.

As Sophia unfolded the crumpled paper, her eyes locked onto the words inscribed in Erica's familiar handwriting.As Sophia read the words penned on that crumpled piece of paper, an overpowering sense of shock and disbelief washed over her. The contents of the letter were beyond imagination, a revelation that struck like a bolt of lightning.

Erica had made a fateful decision, one that would irrevocably alter the trajectory of her life. She had chosen to elope with Roy, a person they had never known. She fell deeply in love with Roy, carried away by the strong currents of affection that had quietly bound them together. Erica felt compelled to be with him, no matter the cost.

In that moment, the room seemed to spin with disorientation. And the Sisterhood found themselves on the precipice of an unfathomable abyss. Sophia's hands quivered as she conveyed the contents of the letter." I've made the most agonizing choice of my life," she read, her words trembling in the room's charged atmosphere.

"We're deeply in love, and we can't bear to be apart any longer. I'm aware that my decision will pierce all of your hearts, especially Elena's. I hope you can find it in your hearts to forgive me someday."
A heavy, stunned silence enveloped the room. Tears welled up in the eyes of Sophia and her companions as they grappled with the enomity of the shocking revelation.

Amidst the rush of wedding arrangements and the excited expectations, they had been caught unawares.The abruptness of it all was overwhelming. Elena, her world shattered by the letter and the painful realization that her sister had vanished from her life stood there paralyzed by pain. Her heartache bled through her sobs; each tear a testament to the pain she could no longer contain.

Her voice quivered with a mixture of anger, grief, and shocking bewilderment. "How could she do this?", she cried out, her anguish echoing in the room's gloomy atmosphere. "Why didn't she confide in me about this? And who in the world is Roy?" Her questions hung in the air, laden with the heavy burden of these unresolved mysteries.

Isabella, summoning every ounce of strength to keep her own emotions in check gently wrapped her arm around Elena's trembling shoulders. "We don't have all the answers, Elena," she murmured softly, her voice infused with unwavering empathy. "But we'll find Erica, and you're not alone in this. We're here for you, no matter what it takes."

The initial shock that had rendered them speechless had now transformed into an unwavering resolve to bring her back home. Upon discovering the letter penned by Erica, Elena and her friends wasted no time in springing into action. The first step was to inform Elena's parents, Mr. Deno Ramirez and Mrs. Roma Ramirez about the calamitous situation.

Amelia took the lead, ushering the Ramirez couple into the room. Their expressions were a cocktail of surprise, confusion, and concern. Their initial surprise was met with the sight of Erica's tear-stained face and the stunned expressions of the rest of the group. With a sense of urgency and realizing the gravity of the situation, Amelia took swift action.

She handed Erica's letter to Mr. Ramirez, placing it directly into his hands. Mr. Ramirez's face contorted with disbelief and anguish as he read Erica's letter, his world crumbling before him. He slumped onto the nearest sofa, the weight of the revelation bearing down on him with an unrelenting force. His anguished cry echoed through the room, a piercing expression of his torment.

Seeing her husband's distress, Mrs. Ramirez gently took the letter from his trembling hands. She began to read it, her expression a mix of dread and sorrow. As the weight of Erica's words settled upon her, tears welled up in her eyes, tracing a heart-breaking path down her cheeks. A loud, grief-stricken cry escaped her lips. And she clutched the letter to her chest, her sobs uncontrollable.

Elena, overwhelmed by her mother's grief, moved to comfort her, wrapping her arms around her and guiding her to sit down on the sofa besides Mr. Ramirez. In a heartfelt embrace, the Ramirez's clung to one another, their tears flowing freely. The depth of their concern and worry for their elder daughter's well-being was casting a shadow over their hearts.

Mrs. Ramirez, her gentle spirit weighed down by sorrow, sobbed deeply as she shared her perspective. "We had our suspicions about Roy right from the start," she confessed, her voice quivering with emotion. "But we didn't want to push Erica away by outright forbidding her to see him. Every time we asked Erica about it, she would deflect the conversation.

She insisted that they were merely good friends." Mr. Ramirez's voice trembled as he recounted the past. "Erica had talked to us about Roy," he began, his brow furrowing with regret. "From the very beginning, I had reservations about Roy. I warned her not to pursue this relationship further, thinking it was just a fleeting college romance.

In our desperation to guide her, we even contemplated arranging her marriage to another man, hoping it would deter her from pursuing this relationship any further. It was during this time that John proposed to her. And to our surprise, she accepted. With the acceptance of John's proposal and Erica's apparent happiness in their relationship, all doubts about Roy seemed to dissipate".

Mr. Ramirez's expression softened as he spoke about John, emphasizing the qualities that had endeared him to their family. "John is not just a good young man, he's someone we genuinely love," Mr. Ramirez remarked, his voice reflecting warmth and affection. "He's the son of my childhood friend, a connection that goes back many years.

John possesses a heart of gold, a kind and compassionate nature that has won over not only Erica but our entire family. He's been a source of strength and support during these challenging times." Elena's voice quivered with a blend of sorrow and frustration as she spoke her mind. "We must inform John," she insisted, her emotions laid bare.

"But I don't think I can summon the strength to face him." Sophia, ever the composed and level-headed one nodded in understanding. "Elena, I'll go and find John," she reassured her friend. "We need to inform him first. And we must also reach out to your extended family, to let them know about this situation." Sophia and Olivia sought out John and ushered him into the room.

John's face bore a mixture of confusion and concern as he surveyed the tearful expressions around him. Sophia guided him to a seat. She placed Erica's letter into John's trembling hands. As John read through Erica's letter, his eyes darted across the lines, absorbing the shocking revelation. He was overwhelmed by an intense wave of grief and disbelief.

John's agony was excruciating, his chest heaving with an angst-ridden sigh that mirrored the overwhelming sadness and turmoil that had taken hold of his heart. The room seemed to vibrate with the sound of that sigh, a heavy and sorrowful note that lingered in the air. The silence that followed stretched on. Finally he found his voice, laced with sadness and a deep sense of self-doubt.

"I always had this nagging feeling," John confessed, his voice distorted with a mix of grief and self-reflection. "That Erica was a star shining in a sky I could never reach. She was way out of my league."A single tear carved a glistening path down John's face, which he tenderly wiped it away with his thumb. Erica enveloped John in a tight embrace.

Her voice trembled with remorse as she apologized." I am so sorry," she whispered. "We're all sorry". But I implore you, please don't let the hatred for Erica consume your heart," Erica earnestly pleaded. "She made a thoughtless decision, a dumb mistake that she will deeply regret." John's response, however was full of love and forgiveness that transcended his pain.

"I could never hate Erica," he declared. "I've loved her for as long as I can remember". After a prolonged silence, he spoke determinedly, "I need to share what has transpired with my parents and family." With a supportive hand from Mr. Ramirez, John rose to his feet. John reached for his phone and dialled his parents, Mr. Chris Silva and Mrs. Crystal Silva.

He requested them to come to the function hall along with the rest of the family. Resolute to face his loved ones, he set off for the hall with Mr. and Mrs. Ramirez walking alongside him. Concerned about the potential reaction of the Silva family upon learning of the situation, Elena tried to dissuade her parents from leaving. Mr. Ramirez countered Elena's concerns.

He emphasized the duty they bore for Erica's actions. "Facing the consequences of Erica's choices is an unavoidable responsibility", he said. John entered the hall followed by the Ramirez family and the Sisterhood. The tension was thick in the air. As John spoke to his parents and family in hushed whispers, a wave of shock and anger rippled through their corner.

The Silva family rushed towards the Ramirez family, their emotions running high. John immediately positioned himself as a buffer between the agitated Silva family and the stunned Ramirez family. He worked to calm the Silva's down understanding the pain and anger that filled their hearts. After a tense exchange, the Silva's, still hurt and furious, departed abruptly.

John, torn between his love for Erica and his duty to his family, shook hands with Mr. Ramirez, his face reflecting the turmoil within. He then followed the Silva's, leaving the Ramirez family standing there, swamped by a sense of shame and sadness. With heavy hearts, Mr. & Mrs. Ramirez retreated to their room besieged by angst and heartache.

The Sisterhood stood transfixed, their expressions a mixture of shock and concern. Hearing the commotion, Miguel, Juan, and Carolina rushed into the room. With a blend of confusion and concern, they scanned the room seeking answers. As Amelia recounted the unfolding events, all three of them stood there, stunned, absorbing the gravity of the situation.

Sophia assumed control, leading everyone to the suite. "We must address this grave situation and come up with a plan," she said firmly. In solemn silence, the eight of them entered the suite, each pondering the next course of action. Miguel spoke up, "What should be our next plan of action?" Carolina suggested, "We should call the police first. Erica's safety is our top priority."

Amelia, the know-it-all of the group, chimed in, "Erica's letter bears her own handwriting. And it seems she's gone away on her own accord. Contacting the police might not bear fruit". "So, what should we do? Just sit here twiddling our thumbs?" Elena, visibly frustrated, exclaimed. "No!", Sophia intervened. "We need to find Erica, but perhaps we should first consider unofficial channels.

Let's try to gather information discreetly and see if we can locate her without involving the authorities just yet". Sophia turned to Elena and inquired, "Elena, your uncle was a police officer in Dubai, right?" Elena nodded, replying, "Yes, Uncle Vincent. Although, he works in the Interpol now." Sophia suggested, "Can we contact him?"

Elena's face lit up with hope. "Yes," she said, "He's come to attend the wedding. I'll call him here." Elena, in a trembling voice, requested Mr. Vincent Gomes to come to their suite. Mr. Gomes stepped inside the suite, his face reflecting bewilderment as he took in the sepulchral atmosphere. "What's going on? Why do you all look so distraught?", he enquired fraught with worry.

Elena attempted to speak but dissolved into sobs. Frustration mounting, Mr. Vincent demanded, "Could someone please explain what's happening here?" Elena, overwhelmed by emotions, struggled to speak. She gestured Sophia to explain. Sophia took a deep breath and began, "Mr. Gomes, we're facing a difficult situation. It's about Erica."

Mr. Vincent's expression grew serious as he listened intently." Erica has eloped with someone named Roy. We're deeply concerned for her safety." Sophia continued," We need your help to locate her, but we can't involve the police officially." Mr. Vincent's eyes widened in surprise and concern. "Tell me everything," he said, his tone now filled with a sense of immediacy.

Sophia, sensing Mr. Vincent's growing concern and willingness to help, went on to explain the entire situation. She detailed how they had discovered Erica's letter explaining her decision, and the confrontation with John and his family. Mr. Vincent listened attentively, his face showing a mix of shock and worry. Sophia finished recounting the events.

"Vincent Uncle, please help us find Erica", cried Elena. Mr. Vincent nodded slowly and said, "We need to act quickly and discreetly to locate Erica. I'll do everything I can to help, but we must keep this unofficial. We don't want to involve the authorities unless absolutely necessary." The Sisterhood nodded silently in agreement.

Mr. Vincent shared, "I have a friend in the Mumbai police force here, ACP Vishal Wagle. He's an honest, non-corrupt, and efficient officer. He's currently suspended for thrashing the local MLA's son who was accused of eve teasing and hooliganism. While he can be a bit hot-headed at times, he's known for his competence and is well respected within the department.

I believe he can assist us discreetly in this matter." Sophia and her friends felt a glimmer of hope as Mr. Vincent mentioned ACP Vishal Wagle. They understood the value of having someone with connections and competence on their side. Elena wiped away her tears and said, "Uncle Vincent, please contact ACP Wagle and explain the delicate situation we're in.

We just want to ensure Erica's safety and bring her back home." Mr. Vincent nodded, "I'll reach out to him immediately, and explain the urgency. Rest assured, we'll do everything we can to locate Erica and ensure her well-being." Mr. Vincent made the call to ACP Vishal Wagle, engaging in a bit of small talk before laying out the sequence of events.

He requested ACP Wagle's immediate presence at the hotel. ACP Wagle assured him that he would reach the hotel shortly. True to his word, ACP Wagle arrived at the hotel, where Mr. Vincent was waiting to receive him. Together, they proceeded to the suite where the Sisterhood and others anxiously awaited their arrival. ACP Vishal Wagle was a striking figure.

He was young and robust, with a well-groomed moustache that added to his commanding presence. His muscular physique hinted at his dedication to physical fitness. He possessed a dusky complexion that only enhanced his rugged handsomeness, making him stand out in any crowd. ACP Vishal Wagle entered the room with an air of authority.

His keen eyes scanned the faces of those gathered. The Sisterhood and the rest of the group couldn't help but be impressed by his imposing yet composed demeanour. Mr. Gomes quickly introduced ACP Wagle to the group, explaining the sequence of events. ACP Wagle listened intently, his moustache twitching as he absorbed the details.

After hearing the entire story, he nodded thoughtfully, "I understand the gravity of this situation." ACP Wagle said in a firm, reassuring tone. "I may be suspended, but I still have contacts and resources. Rest assured, we will do everything we can to locate Erica and ensure her safety. Retired Inspector Govind Ranavde will join us. His network of informers is still active.

Ranavde's extensive network and investigative skills would be our best chance at uncovering the truth and locating Erica. Simmy, a cybercrime specialist will assist in finding the digital clues to trace Erica. Chris, who had been away and had just returned, hurried into the suite. Overwhelmed by sadness upon hearing the news about Erica, he too pledged his support.

Ranavde with his bald head and comfortable potbelly exuded a friendly and approachable demeanour. This put people at ease making it easy for him to gather information from various sources. However, beneath this seemingly unassuming facade, lay a cunning and investigative mind that had honed its skills over years of solving complex cases.

His ability to connect dots and unravel mysteries made him a valuable asset to the team in their quest to find Erica. Simmy, an ethical hacker was the daughter of the notorious cybercriminal, Cheetah99. Despite her young age of 19, she possessed the expertise of a seasoned veteran in the cyber world. Her thin frame and short hair gave her a no-nonsense appearance.

Her journey into the world of hacking had begun at the astonishingly early age of four. Unlike her criminal father, Simmy chose a different path, using her formidable talents to protect and serve the digital realm. Simmy brought a unique set of skills to the team. Her expertise in digital forensics and tracing online activities would prove invaluable in their search for Erica.

As the team of Mr. Vincent, ACP Wagle, Retired Inspector Govind Ranavde, and Simmy gathered in the room, their combined expertise and resources felt like a formidable force. Mr. Vincent addressed the team, "I am sure and confident that this team will be able to locate Erica. Elena, I need to be with your dad at this time of need. I will keep myself updated with the ongoing search.

ACP Wagle's secret headquarters, 'Mount Erebus' was located in the heart of the bustling slums of Dharavi. Dharavi is one of the largest slum areas in Mumbai, India, and is one of the most densely populated places on Earth. The slums are packed with narrow lanes and closely-packed structures leaving little room for open spaces, which made it ideal for their secret headquarters.

The exterior of the place seemed run-down and unassuming blending into the nondescript surroundings. It bore the appearance of neglect and abandonment, with faded paint and weathered walls. However, as one crossed the threshold and stepped inside, a different world unfolded. The interior of the place was unexpectedly spacious and well-equipped.

It was a space that ACP Wagle had chosen for his clandestine operations, a hidden sanctuary for conducting covert investigations and gathering critical intelligence. The headquarters was aptly named Mount Erebus. It was meticulously organized with an array of cutting-edge equipment strategically positioned throughout the headquarters.

Hi-tech computers hummed with activity, their screens displaying intricate networks of information. Wall-mounted screens showcased live feeds from surveillance cameras stationed at key locations across the city. Shelves were lined with reference books, case files, and communication devices, all neatly arranged and easily accessible.

A long, well-lit table served as a central command post. Here, the team would analyse data, plan operations, and coordinate their efforts. In the center of the room, an evidence board took its place, ready to serve as a hub for laying out and connecting the myriad of clues that would guide their investigation. Juan, resourceful as ever, had managed to procure a dozen discreet SIM cards.

These SIM cards would prove invaluable for maintaining secure communications and anonymity during their search. Miguel and Chris, with their technical expertise, took on the task of configuring the high-performance servers and laptop. They meticulously installed the necessary operating system and other hardware and software components.

Now Simmy's hacking station would be fully operational and capable of handling the complex tasks ahead. Simmy watched with anticipation as her hacking station came to life. She had dedicated her life to solving crimes and helping people, and this mission was no exception. She expressed her thanks profusely for the support and assistance of the Sisterhood and their friends.

Suddenly Chris hollered, "You know, they say a bride running away from her own wedding is a rare sight, almost as rare as finding a unicorn! But don't worry, folks, I've checked the stables. No unicorns in sight. We're all good!" Chris' well-timed joke instead of causing offense, diffused the tension in the room, eliciting smiles and a few chuckles from the gathered team.

With the 'Find Erica' headquarters fully operational and abuzz with activity, the team was poised to begin their search for Erica. By utilizing their collective skills and resources, they were ready to uncover the truth and bring Erica back safely. The room hummed with a sense of determination and purpose as they prepared to embark on their mission.

Chapter 4

The Hunt Commences!

Setting up the headquarters for the 'Find Erica' mission had been an arduous task, one that consumed the entire day and stretched well into the night. The room had been transformed into a fully-functioning bustling hub of activity. ACP Vishal Wagle, a man with a reputation for getting the job done, addressed his team, congratulating them on their tireless efforts.

With a sense of camaraderie and shared purpose, the group had worked diligently to assemble the necessary equipment. Simmy, the young cybercrime specialist had configured a state-of-the-art hacking station with the help of Miguel and Chris. The servers were humming with anticipation, ready to sift through digital traces that might lead them to Erica's whereabouts.

With the setup complete, ACP Wagle gathered the team around him. He acknowledged their dedication and commitment, recognizing the importance of the task at hand. "We've taken the first crucial steps," he said, his voice filled with determination. "More than 24 hours have passed since Erica's disappearance, and every moment is crucial.

I urge all of you to get a proper night's sleep. From now on, we may not have many chances for rest until we find Erica." Well-rested, the team assembled at the headquarters the next day, their determination and resolve stronger than ever. ACP Wagle took the lead, addressing the group, "What clues do we have at our disposal?"

"Erica's letter," Sophia replied, holding it up. "It's the most significant piece of information we have right now. Amelia is a handwriting expert. And we can analyse it for hidden insights." Simmy

looked at Amelia, intrigued. "Amelia, you're a handwriting expert?" Amelia nodded, her demeanour calm and confident. "Yes, Simmy, I've been studying handwriting for years." Simmy couldn't help but smile at Amelia's understated expertise.

Simmy watched as Amelia carefully scrutinized the handwriting. "What do you see, Amelia?" Simmy asked, her eyes trained on the paper. Amelia furrowed her brow in concentration. "There's a lot we can glean from handwriting, Simmy," she replied. "For instance, the slant of the letters can indicate a person's emotional state.

Here, I can see that Erica's letters are leaning slightly to the right, suggesting a desire to move forward in life."Amelia pointed to the consistent size of Erica's letters, indicating a person who values balance and harmony. "The spacing is also intriguing," she continued. "Notice how the words are evenly spaced, but there's a slight gap between the lines.

This could suggest that Erica wants to maintain a sense of order but also create some distance, perhaps to protect herself emotionally." We can see that Erica's strokes are moderately heavy. This indicates determination and a strong will. She's someone who is not easily swayed by others."Amelia traced her finger along the curves of Erica's letters.

"There's a sense of fluidity and grace in her handwriting, suggesting a person who is sensitive to beauty and aesthetics. But there's also a hidden tension in the strokes, especially towards the end of the letter. It's as though she was conflicted." Simmy quizzed, "So, what's your overall impression, Amelia?" Amelia set down the letter, her expression thoughtful.

"Erica's handwriting tells us that she's a determined and balanced individual. But there's an underlying conflict that she's not fully expressed in the letter". She took out a magnifying glass and carefully examined Erica's letter once more. "As we discussed earlier," Amelia began, "Erica's handwriting suggests she's a determined individual, but there's an underlying conflict.

Now, let's dive deeper into the content of the letter." She pointed at specific words and phrases as she spoke. "Here, in the beginning, she mentions making the 'most agonizing choice of her life'. This indicates that her choice to run away was not impulsive. It was something she had been grappling with for a while." Simmy leaned closer, her curiosity piqued.

"What about the part where she says, "We're deeply in love, and we can't bear to be apart any longer?" Amelia nodded. "That's crucial, Simmy. It tells us that there's a strong emotional connection between Erica and this person, Roy. The use of 'We're deeply in love' implies the intensity of their love. But remember, it's not just about love.

It's about their inability to be apart which could indicate external pressure or threats." Miguel chimed in, " So, there might be someone or something forcing her into this situation." Amelia agreed. "Exactly, Miguel. Now, look at this, 'I hope you can find it in your hearts to forgive me someday.' This suggests that Erica is torn between her love for her family and her feelings for Roy.

She feels guilty about hurting her loved ones." Sophia added," But what if the part about her family forgiving her is just a cover? What if she's trying to protect them from something more sinister?" The room fell silent as they contemplated Sophia's words. ACP Wagle spoke up, "So, we have a determined Erica with a strong emotional connection to Roy.

But she also has a sense of guilt or obligation toward her family. Our next step is to find out who this Roy is and what kind of influence he has on her." Simmy tapped her fingers on the keyboard, ready to dive into the digital world for any leads on Roy. Despite Simmy's best efforts, there was little she could find about Roy. It seemed like a dead end.

Perhaps Roy was a fake name or he had taken great precautions to remain hidden in the digital realm. Frustration and impatience lingered in the room as they hit a wall in their investigation. However, the team didn't give up. They decided to search Erica's room once more, hoping to uncover any hidden clues that might lead them to Roy's true identity.

As they combed through her belongings, persistence paid off. Tucked away in a forgotten corner of a drawer, they discovered a secret diary. The diary contained Erica's love poems, each filled with her heartfelt emotions for Roy. It was in one of these poems that they found a crucial clue. Erica had described her lover as having a fair face, a chiselled jaw, a lean body.

And her favourite detail, a mole on the right side of his upper lip. It was a breakthrough, a tangible lead to follow. With this newfound information, the team felt a renewed sense of hope and purpose. They were one step closer to identifying Roy and, hopefully, to finding Erica. The mole on the upper lip was a distinctive feature that could prove invaluable in their search.

Erica had been a student at Saint Martin's College in Khar, a prestigious institution known for its academic excellence and vibrant student community. Mr. Ranavde wasted no time in disseminating the description of Roy to his extensive network of informers, hoping to gather any information that could lead them to Roy or Erica's whereabouts.

Meanwhile, the Sisterhood decided to reach out to some of Erica's closest friends from college; Khushboo, Mahi, and Rimjhim. They had known Roy, as Erica had introduced him to them during their tenure at Saint Martin's. However, there was a peculiar detail that made Roy stand out in their memory. He always wore a cap pulled low, obscuring much of his facial features.

Despite this, they managed to catch a glimpse of a distinctive mole on the right side of his upper lip, just as Erica had described in her poem. While Khushboo and Mahi provided valuable information, Rimjhim's behaviour raised red flags. She appeared nervous and evasive during their conversation, giving vague or incomplete answers to their questions.

Her demeanour left Elena and the group feeling uneasy as if there was something she was deliberately withholding. The clues gathered from Khushboo and Mahi, particularly the description of the mole on Roy's upper lip, were promising leads. Still, Rimjhim's behaviour suggested that there might be something more to the story.

But the information gleaned by Mr. Ranavde from his network of informers and his contacts in the police force was nothing short of shocking and deeply unsettling. According to his report, over half a dozen girls had mysteriously gone missing in the past year, all of them running away from their homes under perplexing circumstances.

What sent chills down everyone's spines was that each of these cases shared a common and eerie detail: the presence of a man with a low hat, who seemed to be connected to the disappearances. However, in none of the previous cases was there any mention of the distinctive mole on the right side of the upper lip that Erica had described in her poem about Roy.

This revelation left the group grappling with a disconcerting possibility. Could this elusive man in the low hat be the same Roy that Erica had run away with? If so, why had he chosen to hide this unique facial feature when interacting with other girls? The absence of the mole in the other cases raised more questions than it answered.

As the group pondered the implications of this newfound information, a sense of urgency and dread settled over them. It was clear that they were dealing with a complex and perilous situation that extended beyond Erica's disappearance. The Sisterhood made the decision to reconnect with Erica's friends once more, aiming to delve further into their interactions with Roy.

Khushboo and Mahi arrived at the meetup, but there was no sign of Rimjhim. When inquired about her absence, they revealed that Rimjhim had declined to attend, citing health issues. The Sisterhood couldn't help but find it peculiar that Rimjhim had chosen to skip such a crucial meeting. They proceeded to inquire about how Khushboo and Mahi had first met Roy.

Both girls recounted that their introduction to Roy had been entirely by chance, as they had crossed paths at a local coffee shop. Initially, the encounter had seemed quite ordinary. They hadn't paid particular attention to his appearance. However, things took a peculiar turn when Erica with her characteristic confidence slapped Roy's hand away as he attempted to cover his face.

This unexpected gesture had allowed Khushboo and Mahi to catch a glimpse of the distinctive mole on the right side of Roy's upper lip. It was this unforgettable detail that had etched itself into their memory. But when questioned further about their subsequent encounters with Roy, both girls confessed to having seen him only from a distance on multiple occasions.

He was always in the company of a man named Manek. Manek, they s a i d was Rimjhim's brother, a connection that raised more questions about the mysterious Roy. Why was Roy frequently seen in the company of Rimjhim's brother, Manek? Was there a deeper association between the two that might provide clues about his true identity and motives?

The group recognized that Manek's involvement could be significant. And they decided to investigate this angle further, hoping it would shed light on the enigmatic man they were seeking. Upon reaching out to the college for Rimjhim's address, the Sisterhood was shocked to discover that Rimjhim's credentials and address were fake.

The revelation that Rimjhim had used fake credentials and a fabricated address only deepened the intrigue surrounding her role in Erica's disappearance. It became evident that Rimjhim had gone to great lengths to conceal her true identity. The pieces of the puzzle were slowly coming together, suggesting a possible connection between Rimjhim and Erica's mysterious disappearance.

Khushboo and Mahi's account of Rimjhim's arrival at Saint Martin's College in Khar was a pivotal piece of information.It was revealed that Erica had initially not held a favorable opinion of Rimjhim. It raised questions about how Rimjhim had infiltrated Erica's circle of friends, and what had driven her to befriend Erica despite Erica's reservations about their friendship.

Rimjhim had joined as a transfer student.It hinted at a deliberate strategy to become a part of Erica's life. Simmy was relentless in her pursuit of digital traces related to the suspicious trio. However, her efforts yielded frustratingly minimal results. It seemed as though they had expertly covered their tracks online, leaving behind no discernible digital footprint.

Meanwhile, ACP Wagle and Mr. Ranavde contemplated alternative investigative approaches. They considered reaching out to informants within the criminal underworld who might have knowledge of individuals matching the descriptions provided by Khushboo and Mahi; a man with a mole, Roy; and a mysterious character named Manek.

The day had been filled with frustration and dead ends as the team worked tirelessly to uncover any leads in Erica's disappearance. Hope seemed to be slipping through their fingers. But sometimes, when you least expect it, a glimmer of hope appears in the darkest of moments. Khushboo and Mahi's call came as a surprise. The urgency in their voices was impossible to ignore.

The entire team gathered around, hanging on to every word as the two friends recounted their unexpected encounter. It was a chance meeting that would change the course of their investigation. As Khushboo explained how she and Mahi had gone to meet her friend at Welingkar Institute in Matunga, her voice quivered with a mix of excitement and apprehension.

She described spotting Manek, Rimjhim's brother, a mysterious figure they had heard of but knew so little about. He sat alone in a café, seemingly waiting for someone, his demeanour uneasy. Mahi, her curiosity piqued, decided to approach Manek. She recounted how, when she reached his table, his reaction had been nothing short of startling.

He appeared shocked and perturbed, as if caught off guard. Khushboo joined Mahi at the table. As they both engaged Manek in conversation, they couldn't help but feel that something was amiss. Manek's nervous glances and evasive responses only fuelled their suspicions. It was clear that he was not expecting to be confronted by anyone, let alone Khushboo and Mahi.

He got even more perturbed when they mentioned about Erica. Their attention then shifted to the direction in which Manek had been anxiously glancing. To their astonishment, they spotted Rimjhim making a hasty exit from the café. Rimjhim's sudden departure raised further questions, and they couldn't help but connect the dots.

Khushboo and Mahi were determined not to let this opportunity slip away. They recounted how they had called out to Rimjhim, urging her to stop. Yet, in an instant, she had disappeared into the bustling city lanes. Manek too had slipped away quietly. Amidst the chaotic scene, Khushboo had skilfully snapped photos of both Rimjhim and Manek.

As they shared the photograph of Manek and Rimjhim with the group, their sense of anticipation grew. Simmy took charge of enhancing the image using her expertise to unveil any hidden details. The group watched as the image sharpened, revealing Manek's features more clearly. His dishevelled hair, the scar on his cheek, and a distinct tattoo on his wrist became more evident.

As Rimjhim's image sharpened, they noticed something unusual. The enhanced image revealed a series of faint scars on Rimjhim's hands. These scars were small and easily missed in the original photograph. They raised questions about Rimjhim's past and the possibility of her involvement in activities that could have caused such marks.

Simmy's success in enhancing the photo was met with cheers and a renewed determination to identify Manek. ACP Wagle and Mr. Ranavde quickly disseminated the new image and description to their network of informants hoping to gather more information about this mysterious figure and his potential connection to Erica's disappearance.

The unexpected encounter at the café had breathed new life into their investigation, rekindling the flames of hope. The team was now more resolved than ever to follow this promising lead, wherever it might lead them. The Sisterhood and their allies were prepared to leave no stone unturned in their quest to bring Erica back home safely.

As they dug deeper into the enigma, the team couldn't shake the feeling that there were even more secrets lurking beneath the surface. With each revelation, they realized that they were not only racing against time but also against a cunning and elusive adversary who seemed determined to remain hidden in the shadows.

Chapter 5

A Breakthrough Emerges!

An informant's tip about Manek's location was like a spark in the dark night igniting hope and urgency in the hearts of the team. ACP Vishal Wagle wasted no time. He knew that the clock was ticking, and they couldn't afford any delays. He immediately contacted Commissioner Deb, a man who had known him for years. He provided a detailed account of the events to him.

The Commissioner, sympathetic to ACP Wagle's dedication, gave his consent for the operation. But he had a crucial condition; ACP Wagle couldn't be directly involved due to his suspension. Instead, he was to plan and orchestrate the operation while maintaining a safe distance. With the Commissioner's green light, ACP Wagle sprang into action.

He organized a SWAT team, comprised of highly trained and skilled officers. Each member of the team was a silent warrior, ready to face danger and uncertainty head-on. They gathered at the designated location, geared up and prepared for the operation that would hopefully bring them closer to solving the mystery of Erica's disappearance.

Tembipada, Bhandup, was a labyrinth of narrow lanes and cramped houses, a place where every corner seemed to hide secrets. As the SWAT team made their way through these congested alleys, curious onlookers watched with a mix of amusement and intrigue. The team's presence in their neighbourhood was an unusual sight. The atmosphere was heavy with tension.

With adrenaline pumping through their veins, the SWAT members finally reached the address provided by the informant. The house stood in eerie silence, an unassuming facade for what lay inside.

The team, weapons at the ready, were prepared to breach the door. With precision and swiftness, they broke open the door. The team rushed into the dimly-lit interior. Manek, alerted by the commotion, attempted to make a hasty escape. A heart-pounding chase sequence ensued as Manek darted through the labyrinthine alleys of Tembipada with the SWAT team hot on his heels.

Narrowly squeezing through tight passages, leaping over obstacles, and expertly navigating the maze-like lanes, Manek's flight seemed desperate but determined. The chase was electrifying, a game of cat and mouse that kept everyone on edge. Finally, with a burst of speed, one of the SWAT officers managed to close the gap, lunging forward to apprehend Manek.

And in that split second, Manek's fate was sealed. With a swift and expertly executed manoeuvre, the officer brought him to the ground, restraining him effectively. But the operation held one more surprise. Rimjhim, who had been caught up in the chaos was also apprehended. She stood there, fear and defiance in her eyes, a crucial piece of the puzzle that had finally fallen into place.

As the SWAT team regrouped, having successfully captured Manek and Rimjhim, a collective sigh of relief washed over them. They had taken a significant step forward in their mission to find Erica. Now, with these two key figures in custody, they hoped to unravel the truth behind her disappearance and bring her safely back home.

The team immediately set to work conducting a thorough search of the house,which had already proven to be a treasure trove of unexpected revelations.The initial surprise of capturing the two suspects was about to be surpassed by an even more astonishing discovery. Hidden within the confines of the house were numerous documents, meticulously forged and carefully concealed.

The documents were like pieces of a jigsaw puzzle, each one revealing a small part of the larger picture. As the investigators sifted through the trove of forged documents and credentials, their expressions shifted from surprise to bewilderment. It became evident that Manek's real name wasn't Manek at all. Rimjhim was an alias as well.

The fake documents, as deceptive as they were, painted a clearer picture of their true identities, or rather, the lack thereof. Fake passports, counterfeit Aadhar cards, forged certificates, and an array of other fabricated records were meticulously crafted to conceal their true selves. The question that hung in the air was clear – who were these individuals, and what were they hiding?

While Manek and Rimjhim sat in custody, their true identities remained a well-guarded secret buried beneath layers of deception. The Sisterhood, ACP Wagle, Mr. Ranavde, and Simmy knew that they had stumbled upon a significant breakthrough, one that would take them closer to Erica's location and uncover the truth behind her disappearance.

The interrogation room, notorious within the law enforcement community, bore the dark legacy of countless criminals who had passed through its doors. The interrogation room, aptly named 'Tartarus', struck fear into the hearts of criminals. It was whispered that the very walls of the room were painted with the echoes of agonizing cries and desperate pleas for mercy.

The Sisterhood had accidentally ventured into the room once. And the experience had left an indelible mark on their memories. They vowed never to return unless it was absolutely necessary. Manek, now in custody, found himself within the bleak confines of this infamous chamber. Rimjhim, his partner in deception, observed the proceedings from behind a one-way mirror.

She would be a mute spectator, unable to intervene or escape the sounds that would soon emanate from within. The team, initially attempting a good cop-bad cop routine quickly realized that Manek was not an ordinary criminal. His deadpan demeanour and sardonic responses hinted at a resilience that was anything but typical. The first question posed to him was a simple one – his name.

Manek, with a wry smile, replied with a quote attributed to Shakespeare: "What's in a name?" Senior Inspector Srilakshmi, renowned for her unyielding resolve and sharp wit, leaned forward in her chair, her piercing gaze fixed on Manek. She was often described as the 'Tough-as-Nails Lady Cop'. This was a reputation she had earned through years of relentless pursuit of justice.

Rumours about her abilities abounded, some even suggesting that she could make the dead quote Shakespeare if she wanted to. The thought of such a peculiar talent brought a subtle smile to her face as she listened to Manek's initial retort. In the dimly-illuminated interrogation room, the atmosphere was fraught with tension. Srilakshmi's demeanour remained composed.

She understood that the situation required more than just physical force. It demanded a psychological finesse that she had honed over the years. As Manek quipped with Shakespearean eloquence, Srilakshmi couldn't help but appreciate the cleverness of his response. Her reputation for tenacity was well-deserved. She recognized a worthy adversary in Manek.

However, she also knew that the real test lay ahead, not in verbal sparring, but in unravelling the intricate web of deception that surrounded Erica's disappearance. SI Srilakshmi, renowned for her unyielding determination decided to escalate the interrogation. She delved into the realm of "third-degree," a term synonymous with torture in India.

The room bore witness to a series of increasingly intense techniques aimed at extracting information. Manek's body was laid on cold slabs of ice, his body shivering as the icy chill seeped into his skin. This method wasn't physically painful, but it was psychologically distressing. The biting cold made it difficult for him to concentrate or maintain his composure.

Minutes felt like hours. Manek's sighs of agony echoed through the room, sending chills down the spines of those who were present. It was a haunting sound, a testament to the mental torment he was enduring. Manek was then abruptly pulled away from the frigid slabs of ice. And as they were removed, he was tightly wrapped in layers of warm blankets.

Initially, he felt a sense of relief as his freezing ordeal ended, but little did he know that the room's temperature was about to be raised significantly. As the heat began to rise slowly, it quickly became unbearable for Manek. Beads of sweat formed on his forehead. He started perspiring profusely. Sweat trickled down his face like rivulets.

Strange, guttural sounds emanated from his mouth, startling everyone who heard them. The transformation from extreme cold to stifling heat was taking a toll on him, both physically and mentally. Meanwhile, Rimjhim, who was observing the proceedings from her position in the air-conditioned room was also feeling the effects of the intense heat.

Despite being in an air-conditioned environment, the tension, anxiety, and pain in the room seemed to seep through the walls causing her to perspire copiously.The temperature was brought down and the blankets were removed. But Manek's ordeal continued as his eardrums were relentlessly assailed by a cacophony of jarring noises.

It was as if every unpleasant sound had conspired to create an auditory assault, the sole purpose of which was to break his will. The symphony of torment included blaring sirens, screeching metal, and the shrill cries of animals. Intermittent bursts of high-pitched laughter followed by deafening explosions shattered the relative silence between these torturous sounds.

It was a maddening cacophony that drilled into Manek's psyche, making rational thought nearly impossible.Each noise seemed to amplify the discomfort caused by the previous one. Manek's senses were overwhelmed. The assault on his ears was both physical and psychological, leaving him disoriented, disheartened, and desperate for it to end.

The tormentors showed no mercy. The relentless noise continued to reverberate within the chamber, a relentless reminder of the lengths to which they were willing to go to break his resolve. Rimjhim, seated in the adjacent room had her hands tightly covering her ears throughout the auditory assault, desperately trying to shield herself from the relentless onslaught of noise.

The excruciating sounds still managed to penetrate her senses making her experience the torment vicariously. It was an excruciating ordeal for all involved. The room resonated with a symphony of suffering that seemed never-ending. The relentless auditory assault had become unbearable even for the Sisterhood. They couldn't endure the torment any longer.

Overwhelmed by the discomfort and moral unease, they hastily rushed out of the room. In the dimly-lit confines of the interrogation room, the seasoned law enforcement officers, Srilakshmi and Wagle, exchanged knowing glances. They harboured no illusions about extracting valuable information from Manek, the resilient criminal who had proven himself to be a formidable adversary.

Their true target, they understood was the apprehensive figure on the other side of the one-way mirror; Rimjhim.As she watched and listened from the safety of her concealed vantage point, the weight of her complicity in the unfolding drama bore down on her. Both Srilakshmi and Wagle were keenly aware that it was only a matter of time before Rimjhim's resolve began to crumble.

Her loyalty to Manek and her own involvement in the elaborate charade were vulnerabilities they intended to exploit. They knew that psychological pressure, rather than physical torture, would be the key to unlocking the truth. As Manek endured the physical torture, Rimjhim was subjected to intense psychological torment. Her unease grew with each passing moment.

ACP Wagle and SI Srilakshmi were well aware that her mental fortitude was beginning to collapse under the pressure. The psychological torture inflicted on her was proving to be as effective as any physical method. They could see that it was only a matter of time before she would be compelled to reveal the information they sought.

The room was filled with the agonizing screams of Manek as heavy logs were placed on his body and rolled over him, inflicting intense pain. Rimjhim, unable to bear witness to this brutality any longer, broke down into tears, covering her ears and pleading for the torment to stop. The relentless torture had pushed her to the brink.

Her desperation to end the suffering became evident. Rimjhim's plea echoed in the room, her trembling voice carrying the weight of the secrets she held. It was a pivotal moment in the interrogation, as her willingness to cooperate hung in the balance. With Rimjhim's plea to stop the torture, it was evident that she had reached her breaking point.

The relentless and brutal methods had shattered her resolve. She was now willing to talk. This marked a significant breakthrough in their pursuit of answers. SI Srilakshmi and ACP Wagle recognizing the critical moment they had reached, immediately halted the torture and instructed their team to treat Manek's injuries. It was now time to extract information from Rimjhim.

She held the key to understanding Erica's disappearance and uncovering the larger criminal network involved. Rimjhim was given a moment to compose herself before they began the process of questioning her. Rimjhim sat in the interrogation room, her eyes showing a mix of fear, remorse, and resignation. Across from her, sat SI Lakshmi, and ACP Wagle.

The Sisterhood and others observed from behind the one-way mirror. They awaited to hear her account of the events, eager to uncover more about Manek's criminal activities and Erica's whereabouts. Rimjhim showed no resistance or any need for coercion. She began to divulge the painful details of her life with Manek.

As Rimjhim began to reveal her story, the room fell into an uneasy silence. She admitted her real name was Maya and not Rimjhim. Her admission that Manek was not her brother but her husband stunned everyone present. Maya, now openly sharing her painful past, continued with her story. She hailed from a small village in Garhwal, Jalapur, where she had lived a simple life.

It was at a village fair that she had first encountered Manek. He went by Ramesh at the time. At the fair, he had presented himself as an entirely different person. His charm and financial resources had won her heart. Their fairytale romance had led to elopement and getting married. However, Maya's happiness had been short-lived.

She soon discovered the darker side of Ramesh, who was involved in criminal activities. Confronting him led to threats of being sold to a brothel, a horrifying fate that she did not want to endure. She pleaded with him, her eyes filled with desperation, to refrain from doing so. In a moment of apparent mercy, Ramesh offered her an alternative.

He asked her to return to her family. But Maya knew that the shame of eloping with a man would likely lead to her family's rejection. She felt trapped. Her only option seemed to be assisting Ramesh in his criminal endeavours. Maya's narrative painted a picture of a young woman who had been manipulated and coerced into a life she had never imagined.

It was a heart-breaking story that elicited sympathy from some and anger toward Manek from others in the room. However, they were also aware that Maya had become involved in criminal activities alongside Manek. Her cooperation could be vital in dismantling their operations. Their true mission was to build a strong case against the criminal network.

"How did you help him in his criminal activities?", SI Lakshmi probed. "Manek or Ramesh as he was known to me then involved me in various ways", Maya said. "At first, it was simple tasks like running errands and delivering messages. I didn't know the full extent of his illegal activities until later." Maya wiped away her tears, her voice trembling with regret.

"I didn't want to do any of this, but I felt trapped," she confessed. "Manek convinced me that we had no other option. There was no escaping this criminal world. He convinced me that I had to help him or face dire consequences." Maya went on to describe how Manek had trained her in identifying vulnerable targets and gaining their trust.

She would befriend these girls, weaving tales of Manek's kindness and generosity, making them believe that he was their saviour. When the time was right, she would introduce them to Manek. The girls would often fall for his charm immediately. Tears streamed down Maya's face as she spoke, her voice trembling with remorse.

"I became an accomplice in Manek's cruel game," she admitted with a heavy heart. "Once the girls had fallen for his charm and believed in his false promises, I would help them elope with him. It was as though I was leading them into a trap. Their lives would be swept into a relentless whirlpool of misery, where escape seemed impossible".

She explained how these girls would be eventually sold to brothels. Knowing that returning to their families was not an option as their families would never accept them back, they would stay put.

Inevitably, the girls would resign themselves to their fate, however unwillingly.Maya's involvement in this malicious trade had caused immeasurable suffering to countless young lives.

"What was your modus operandi?", questioned ACP Wagle. Maya described, "Our schemes unfolded in countless villages across rural India, where millions of vulnerable girls presented opportunities for our nefarious schemes. To gain their trust, I assumed the role of a sympathetic social worker infiltrating these close-knit communities.

Our sinister charade typically began just before the village fair, an event that provided the ideal cover for our deceptions. I would befriend these unsuspecting girls, feigning empathy. I would then gradually manipulate them with promises of a better future. The village fair, with its bustling crowds and distractions served as the perfect backdrop for our introduction of Manek.

His charisma easily captivated the young minds we targeted. He lured them further into our web of deceit. Amidst the fair's joy and celebration, our malicious intentions remained hidden, forever changing the lives of the innocent girls we ensnared. SI Lakshmi and ACP Wagle exchanged glances, their faces a mirror of shared shock and horror.

"Tell me about Roy.What's his real name? How did you meet him? How did you come to Mumbai?", SI Lakshmi grilled. Maya said, "Roy's real name remains a closely-guarded secret. I do not know his real name. Our encounter with Roy was a twist of fate, born out of the sordid world of gambling and deceit that Manek had become deeply embroiled in".

Maya recalled her first glimpse of Roy in the dimly-lit, smoke-filled atmosphere of a gambling den, a place where fortunes were won and lost, and where desperate souls sought both wealth and escape. It was during one of Manek's many high-stakes gambling sessions that he first crossed paths with Roy. Money was pouring into Manek's pockets through his illicit schemes.

And he became increasingly addicted to the vices of drinking and gambling.On that pivotal night, Manek's streak of good fortune seemed unending. He found himself continuously outwitting Roy in their gambling exchanges. Confidence swelled within him. He began to place substantial bets, convinced that he held the upper hand.

Unbeknownst to Manek, this was a classic manoeuvre in the gambler's playbook, designed to lure the victim into a false sense of security before ruthlessly taking away everything they had. In a cruel twist of fate, the tables were turned on Manek. He ended up losing not only his amassed wealth but also the woman who had become deeply entangled in his life; Maya.

Maya, whose involvement in Manek's schemes had become crucial, suddenly found herself in a precarious position. Manek, cognizant of the fact that he couldn't execute his elaborate plans without her, faced a dilemma. It was then that Roy with his enticing proposition entered the scene. Roy proposed a radical solution for both Manek and Maya.

They were to relocate to Mumbai and collaborate on his criminal enterprise. In return for their participation, Roy promised to absolve Manek's crippling debt and open the doors to even greater riches. Roy unveiled the chilling details of his plan, which revolved around the heartless world of female trafficking. The girls they targeted would be ruthlessly sold to the highest bidder.

Maya, grappling with a sense of morality questioned Roy about the horrific fate that awaited these innocent girls. His callous response was devoid of empathy. "Slavery, torture, death. Who cares? We're only after the money." Maya's eyes glistened with tears as she recounted the cold-hearted indifference that Roy displayed toward the suffering of those they exploited.

Chapter 6

The Truth is Revealed

Maya's revelation sent a shiver of dread through the room. The realization that Erica had been ensnared by a female trafficking syndicate filled them with a sense of urgency and dread. The Sisterhood, ACP Wagle, and SI Srilakshmi were determined to uncover each and every detail of Maya's involvement in these heinous operations.

Their unwavering purpose was to ensure Erica's safe return. The room was fraught with tension as they pressed Maya for more information. SI Srilakshmi leaned forward, her eyes locking onto Maya's, her voice steady yet laced with intensity. "Maya, we need to understand your modus operandi in Mumbai," she began, her words punctuating the gravity of the situation.

"How did you lure these girls into your web? How many of them did you traffic?" It was a critical question. Maya revealed that her approach varied, depending on the circumstances and the vulnerability of her targets. At times, she posed as a fellow student with fabricated credentials, blending seamlessly into the college environment.

On other occasions, she assumed the role of a teacher, her persuasive charm granting her access to unsuspecting victims. And, when necessary, she presented herself as a counsellor, exploiting the trust that girls and their families placed in her guidance. Each role she played came with a meticulously crafted fake identity, complete with forged names and certificates.

The Sisterhood and the law enforcement officers were left in awe of the level of deceit and cunning involved in Maya's schemes. Maya continued her harrowing narrative, providing details about the names and stories she had woven to manipulate her victims.

As she spoke, it became apparent that she had befriended numerous girls, using their vulnerability and trust to lead them into the clutches of the traffickers. Maya's role was integral in the recruitment process. The room remained silent, save for Maya's remorseful confession. The questions loomed heavy, echoing in the minds of those present.

How many innocent lives had been irreparably damaged by Maya's cunning and the malevolent forces she served? The pursuit of justice for Erica had now expanded to encompass a desperate search for the other girls ensnared in this cruel enterprise. The clock continued to tick, relentless in its reminder of the urgency of their mission.

Maya's disturbing narrative unveiled a despicable modus operandi that preyed on the dreams and vulnerabilities of young girls. Maya described how she meticulously portrayed Roy to the unsuspecting girls, skilfully adapting her storytelling to each victim's background. Roy became the knight in shining armour, the embodiment of every romantic ideal they had ever harboured.

He was more than just charming; a handsome man with chiselled features and a captivating smile that could brighten any room. He possessed the looks of a Greek god, a physical allure that made it impossible for these young women to resist his advances. To these girls longed for love in their lives, Roy appeared to be the answer to their prayers.

The girls were completely taken in, falling for his charm, wit, and charisma hook, line, and sinker. Roy's method of operation was not only cunning but also ruthlessly efficient, exploiting the deep-seated fears and values of the girls. Roy, it seemed, had mastered the art of psychological warfare. Maya's aid provided him an additional advantage.

Once he identified a vulnerable girl and began a relationship with her, he would subtly and gradually introduce the idea of marrying her. This was done with such finesse that the girl would agree, even if they had to elope with him. Roy's charm would compel them to obey his every command. Roy's slyness extended to a subtler form of manipulation as well.

Once he had established a relationship with a vulnerable girl, he would cleverly, from the periphery, insinuate to her family that he was not a trustworthy man, subtly sowing seeds of doubt about his true intentions. This indirect approach was designed to make the families believe that they needed to take swift action to safeguard their daughter's future.

In response to Roy's calculated hints and warnings, the families would hasten their wedding plans, convinced that they were acting in their daughter's best interest. This rush to arrange weddings was driven by the genuine concern of the parents. They were led to believe that they were shielding their daughters from potential harm befalling them.

Little did they know that they were unwittingly falling into Roy's trap, as he skilfully exploited their fears and anxieties.He would then unveil the ultimate step of his diabolical plan.He would manipulate the girls into believing that eloping with him on the wedding day itself was their only option, convincing them that it was a grand romantic gesture.

Their love, he would tell them, transcended societal norms. And they deserved to be together at any cost. The wedding day, a symbol of joy and union for most became a day of betrayal and heartache for these unsuspecting girls.Roy's compelling influence would drive them to abandon their families, their dreams of a traditional wedding shattered.

The shame and humiliation of their daughters eloping on the very day they were supposed to be wed would deter the families from pursuing a police case. Roy's cunning manipulation and the genuine letters left behind by the distraught girls would further solidify the illusion that their love was genuine. Maya's role in this vicious operation was crucial.

She would assist the girls in eloping, ensuring that they were placed in a car driven by Manek. This initial journey was fraught with anxiety as the girls had no inkling of the horrors that lay ahead. Manek would transport them to a clandestine exchange point, where Roy would pick them up. He would stay with the victims for a few days until the heat from their disappearances had dissipated.

His shrewd plan then involved orchestrating a sham wedding attended by his so-called best friends, Manek and Maya. The girl would then be persuaded to inform her parents about the marriage. The sudden revelation would land like a thunderbolt in the heart of the girl's family. Such an abrupt declaration would inevitably ignite a firestorm of anger and resentment within the family.

The situation would often escalate into heated and bitter spats. The ensuing chaos and heated arguments would lead the girl to vehemently declare her desire never to lay eyes on her parents again; a scenario that Roy secretly craved. After this tumultuous turn of events, Rimjhim's role in the scheme came to a close. Her part in the plan had served its purpose.

Roy would skilfully manipulate the situation, persuading them that their lives were in grave danger, compelling them to part ways, and arrange a clandestine meeting at an undisclosed location. Manek would escort the girls to a secret location; a safe house. They would wait, trusting that Roy would arrive soon. The syndicate goons would then forcibly pick them up.

The startled girls were then transported to a menacing bidding ground where their fates would be determined by the highest bidder. Beyond this point, Maya admitted, she remained in the dark, unaware of what transpired next. It was a stark revelation that showcased the depths of depravity within this malicious trafficking ring.

Erica's disappearance had led them into the darkest corners of human cruelty. SI Lakshmi's stern gaze bore down on Maya as she demanded answers about Erica. Maya hesitated for a moment, then began to speak, "Erica was never our initial target," Maya confessed. "Our primary focus had been Mahi. I had discreetly captured a photograph of her to be handed over to Roy's boss.

However, fate had its way, as that photograph inadvertently

included Erica. In a pivotal twist, Roy's boss made the momentous decision to change the target to Erica, altering the course of our plan significantly." Maya continued, her voice trembling slightly, "The reason for this change was that one of their clients had an intense desire for Erica after viewing her photograph.

The astonishing offer on the table amounted to a staggering one million dollars, an opportunity too lucrative to resist. The prospect of such immense wealth made us all greedy. And we succumbed to the temptation. But Erica was not an easy target. She possessed a kind of strength and confidence that set her apart." The first step in their plan was for Maya to befriend Erica.

Using a fake identity, Maya infiltrated Erica's life as a fellow student, Rimjhim. She quickly forged a deep friendship with Erica. Although Erica had initial reservations about her, she swiftly worked her way into Erica's confidence, cementing a strong and unbreakable connection between them. She played the role of a trusted confidante gaining Erica's trust over time.

This was the foundation upon which the entire scheme rested. The next crucial step involved Roy's entrance into the unfolding plan. Maya and Roy's initial attempt to use Roy's Greek God looks to ensnare Erica into their scheme proved surprisingly unsuccessful.Erica, a woman of substance, saw through the superficial façade and showed little interest in such attributes.

This unexpected turn prompted Maya to rethink their strategy. Determined to find a way into Erica's heart, Maya delved into her secrets. It was in the midst of one of their heartfelt conversations that Maya uncovered Erica's love for aiding children and her unwavering compassion for stray dogs. This revelation emerged as the cornerstone of their fresh approach and strategy.

Maya seized the opportunity to exploit Erica's passion for philanthropy. She artfully fabricated a pretext to bring Erica to an orphanage, a location she was aware would provide the perfect opportunity to strategically reintroduce Roy into their plan. There, Roy played the role of a caring and responsible individual who seemed genuinely committed to taking care of the children.

In reality, he had merely enticed the children with the promise of chocolates, encouraging them to follow a scripted behaviour as part of the scheme. Erica, witnessing Roy's seemingly selfless act was genuinely impressed by his dedication to children. His performance, though deceptive, resonated with her compassionate nature.

One day as Maya and Erica were strolling through a neighbourhood, they came across Roy feeding food to stray dogs. The sight of Roy's compassion for these vulnerable animals resonated deeply with her. His gesture of providing sustenance and care to the stray dogs mirrored her own love for helping those in need.

Erica saw Roy in a new light, appreciating his empathy and kindness towards animals. Little did she know that this display of kindness was merely another facet of the meticulously orchestrated deception, a web of deceit and peril that would ensnare her in its intricate design. As days turned into weeks, the intricate dance of deception continued.

As she gradually found herself falling in love with him, Roy applied his well-practiced strategy on Erica, exploiting her feelings to further his devious plan. However, in stark contrast to the countless girls who had preceded her, Erica presented a formidable challenge. She was resolute in her refusal to elope, displaying a strength of character they hadn't encountered before.

Instead, she expressed her desire for Roy to meet her parents and gain their approval. This unexpected turn of events was the polar opposite of what Roy had meticulously planned, leaving him in a vulnerable and precarious situation. Erica's determination to introduce Roy to her family was a stark departure from the clandestine elopements he had orchestrated in the past.

It was clear that Erica wanted a genuine and open relationship unlike the secretive affairs Roy was accustomed to. This divergence from the plan set off alarm bells for Roy. He had to think on his feet to maintain his façade. Nevertheless, a pivotal moment unfolded when Erica inadvertently discovered Roy in the act of bribing children with chocolates to stage a performance.

Erica witnessed this damning act unbeknownst to Roy. This sowed a seed of doubt in Erica's mind. His steadfast refusal to meet her parents, his reluctance to reveal himself to her friends, and his unwavering insistence on eloping only deepened Erica's suspicions and doubts about him. She began to question the sincerity of the man she had fallen for.

The realization that Roy might be using manipulation to win her over began to take root. The final blow to their scheme came when Erica witnessed a heart-wrenching scene. She chanced upon Roy brutally kicking a stray puppy, causing it to whimper in pain. The juxtaposition of this cruel act against the kindness he had displayed earlier shattered the illusion Erica had of him.

The sight of Roy laughing while the innocent puppy suffered was a revelation that struck her to the core. Erica confronted him, her eyes filled with disbelief and anger. She severed all ties with him finally seeing through the facade of his charm and kindness. It was at this moment that Maya realized that their meticulously-crafted plan had unravelled.

They were facing not only the loss of a significant sum of money but also the wrath of their dangerous bosses. Desperate and cornered, Maya and Roy were now caught in a perilous web of their own making. The magnitude of their failure and the dire consequences that awaited them hung heavy in the air. Their lives were now in jeopardy.

The unforgiving world of crime they had been entangled in began to close in around them. They were in desperate need of a solution. Their bosses would not take kindly to such a failure. This disclosure sent shockwaves through the room, leaving the group and the officers stunned. Erica's determination to sever all ties with Roy had been clear.

The question of what could have then compelled Erica to elope with him puzzled everyone. SI Lakshmi, her voice tinged with a mix of disbelief and curiosity asked Maya to explain further. Maya began to elaborate, "Roy always had a backup plan. He would discreetly film his private moments with the girls preserving intimate scenes on video.

He needed a leverage to force the girls in case they had second thoughts about their elopement. It was a ruthless insurance policy, a means to ensure they wouldn't back out." Maya continued, "In the case of the first six girls, Roy never had to resort to using those compromising videos. Roy's manipulation was enough to keep them entangled in his web of deceit.

But with Erica, he had to gamble on this option. The covert meetings at the Taj Hotel had become the backdrop for Erica's torment. Roy's relentless threats to expose their relationship to both the groom's family and Erica's own family had pushed her to the brink of despair. Despite the mounting pressure, Erica refused to yield".

Then came the chilling turning point — Roy's ultimate gambit. Roy had one last card to play. "As a last resort," she explained,

"Roy exhorted her to meet him one final time, promising that he would leave her alone afterward." However, in this meeting, Roy unleashed a horrifying revelation. He showed Erica the damning video, exposing the depth of his deceit and manipulation.

The shock of the video's contents left Erica reeling. Roy's threat to publicly play this video on her wedding day, masquerading it as a twisted gift from him was a cruel and calculated move. Unable to bear the weight of the blackmail and fearing the consequences of the video's exposure, Erica broke down. Desperation drove her to beg Roy to delete the incriminating footage.

In the face of Roy's damning video he held as a weapon, Erica found herself cornered and trapped. She felt the walls closing in on her with no escape from this nightmarish ordeal. The weight of her family's honour pressed upon her, leaving her with seemingly no viable alternatives. With a heavy heart and a sense of resignation, Erica reluctantly agreed to Roy's sinister plan.

Her acquiescence was a grim testament to the psychological torment she endured, as well as the dire consequences she sought to avoid. In the shadows of secrecy, Roy outlined his final instructions. He instructed Erica to pen a letter using the exact words he provided carefully crafting it to convey her intention to elope with him. With no alternative, Erica reluctantly acquiesced.

This letter would become both her farewell to her family and her commitment to this twisted plan. Erica would then vanish in the early morning hours of her wedding night. She had to leave behind her bewildered family, her unsuspecting groom, and the life she had once envisioned. The revelation of Erica's harrowing ordeal struck a chord deep within the hearts of those present.

Elena's tears and inconsolable weeping echoed the shared anguish and empathy that engulfed the room. The magnitude of Erica's suffering and her incredible resilience in the face of such adversity left everyone deeply moved. As Elena's sobs filled the air, the room became a muted tableau of grief and compassion. "Oh my god. She had to endure so much pain".

Elena's exclamation echoed the collective sentiment in the room. The depths of Erica's suffering, endured in silence and isolation were almost unimaginable. "I couldn't do anything to help her," Elena cried, her voice filled with regret and sorrow. The others, their own emotions raw and turbulent found themselves torn between their own tears and the urge to console Elena.

"Where is Erica? What happened to her? Where is Roy?", questioned ACP Wagle. "I do not know", Maya whispered. "What do you mean you do not know?", SI Srilakshmi demanded, her frustration evident as she delivered a sharp slap to Maya. Maya sobbed, "Roy did not want to take any chances". Maya elaborated, "Roy changed the plan.

He had prohibited our involvement in the final stages of the operation. He intended to personally collect Erica and transport her to the secret location. He planned to stay with her until they reached the elusive bidding location. But since that night, he has not been in contact with us. That fateful day when Khushboo and Mahi saw us, we were looking out for Roy.

He hung around Matunga Circle colleges and the nearby cafes when he was alone. That's why we were hiding in Tembipada, away from the eyes of police and especially our bosses. "Where was Roy's secret location?", asked SI Lakshmi. "Roy never mentioned it. As Manek dropped off the car and the girl at the Badlapur bridge, Roy would swap the car keys for the bike keys.

Once this exchange was complete, Roy would take possession of the car and leave. Manek's task was to then discreetly ride it to a location near Badlapur Railway Station. There, he would park the bike and seamlessly blend into the crowd of commuters, making his way back home via train. On one particular night driven by a gnawing curiosity, Manek decided to tail Roy discreetly.

As Manek discreetly tailed Roy's car, they ventured deeper into unknown terrain. Finally, Roy arrived at a secluded farmhouse. He swiftly entered the premises, closing the imposing gates behind him. Manek's sharp instincts led him to surmise that this farmhouse was likely situated near Kasara, given the proximity of the Kasara Railway Station".

The sudden disappearance of Roy left everyone involved in the investigation perplexed and anxious. They had seemingly lost hope of finding any leads to Erica or uncovering the truth behind the trafficking operation. However, their fortunes took a turn when the discovery of the farmhouse near Kasara came to light.

Chapter 7

A Sudden Twist!

The night was shrouded in darkness as the mysterious figure, dressed in a red t-shirt and cap got into his car and drove away. The engine's soft hum was the only sound that broke the silence of the deserted road. The journey seemed endless, with winding roads and overhanging trees that blocked out the feeble moonlight. Finally, after what felt like hours, he reached his destination.

It was an old, dilapidated farmhouse standing in eerie isolation. Its decaying facade and overgrown garden gave it an ominous presence, like a relic from a forgotten past. The figure parked his car just inside the rusted iron gate and got out. With cautious steps, he approached the house, the creaking floorboards echoing in the stillness of the night.

The pale glow of his flashlight cut through the darkness, guiding his way. He made his way through the crumbling hallway, his heart pounding with anticipation. In the furthermost corner of the house, he opened a door that led to a dimly-lit room. The faint silhouette of a girl slumped in a chair came into view. The figure moved closer and shone his flashlight on her.

It was Erica, her once vibrant spirit reduced to a shabby and dishevelled form. She slowly opened her eyes, her voice trembling as she spoke, "Who are you? Why are you doing this? Please let me go." The stranger, his face hidden in the shadows of his cap, remained silent. The room seemed to close in around them, and an air of dread hung heavy in the stale, musty air.

The stranger's voice quivered, laden with a deep well of sorrow and frustration, as he began to respond to Erica's desperate pleas. "I've loved you since our childhood", he confessed, the weight of his feelings evident in every word.

You never noticed me all those years, but in these chaotic and perilous times, I came to your rescue". His eyes, concealed by the shadow of his cap, betrayed the intensity of the emotions he had been nurturing in silence. As he continued, the room seemed to hang on his every word. "I saw you that night, hurriedly leaving the Taj in the dead of night.

I rushed into your room. And there it was — your letter. As I read it, shock washed over me. How could my Erica choose to elope with an utterly worthless man? I couldn't simply stand by and allow this to happen", he continued, his voice quivering with a sense of helplessness. He was opening up the emotions he had buried deep within himself for years.

"I followed you to the Hanging Gardens where you met Roy. I saw you talking to that worthless man. I watched from a distance, afraid to intervene, unsure of how to protect you. But then, the argument escalated, and he struck you. You fell unconscious", the stranger continued, his voice taking on a subdued tone as he recollected the events of that fateful night.

"I wanted to confront that man, even hurt him for what he had done to you. But he quickly placed you in his car and sped away. I followed his car driven by a mix of fear and anger. We drove for what seemed like an eternity through unfamiliar terrain until he finally stopped at the gates of this farmhouse. He then got down to open the gates".

The stranger's voice trembled as he recounted the pivotal moment that changed the course of their lives forever. "He opened the gates and let his car in. After letting his car in, he got down to close the gates. I seized that moment, the moment that would alter everything. I snuck up behind him." His voice quivered as he spoke the next words.

"And then, I struck him with a baseball bat. He crumpled to the ground, lifeless, right there." Tears streamed down the stranger's face as he continued his painful admission. "I was terrified," he confessed, his voice trembling. "I had killed a man. The weight of that act was crushing me. But I did it for love. I did it for you." He paused for a moment, trying to compose himself.

"I took you out of the car and laid you on the couch inside the house. You were still unconscious. I was desperate to ensure you were okay. I cleaned your head wounds as gently as I could and let you rest, praying that you would wake up soon." The stranger's voice shuddered with emotion as he added, "Then, I had to confront the grim reality of what I had done.

I needed to get rid of Roy's body to protect you and myself. It was a horrifying task, but I felt I had no other choice." With a mixture of remorse and determination in his voice, the stranger continued his chilling confession. "I dug up a hole in the backyard. The task was gruelling, but the drizzle had softened the ground somewhat, making it marginally easier.

I dragged his lifeless body and unceremoniously deposited it into the pit." His voice took on a tone of defiance as he added, "Before I covered the body with earth, I spat on his face. I was no longer gripped by fear. I had done what I believed was necessary to protect you, Erica, regardless of the consequences. It was my duty to protect you, my Erica".

He hesitated, his voice quivering as he recounted the events of that night. "I came back to check on you. I was exhausted. My clothes were stained with blood and mud. But the weight of what I had done weighed even heavier on my conscience. And then, in your unconscious state, you uttered a name; a name that fills me with anger and resentment to this day."

His voice trembled with a mix of frustration and despair as he continued, "You muttered his name, Erica. You cried, 'John, you came to save me. I am sorry, John. I love you, John.' It felt like a dagger through my heart. My blood boiled with anger and jealousy, but I couldn't bring myself to harm you. So, I tied you to this chair and left you here.

In the depths of my heart, I held onto the hope that one day you would come to realize that your true love is me. Do you recognize me?", yelled the stranger, his voice tinged with hope and anxiety. He continued, "I kept coming back to feed you, to clean you, to watch over you. Do you recognize my touch, Erica?" His eyes searched hers for a glimmer of recognition.

He yearned for a connection to bridge the gap of time and pain that had separated them. Erica, in shock and disbelief, muttered, "Chris?" Her voice shivered as she struggled to comprehend the surreal situation, she found herself in. Tears welled up in Chris' eyes as he nodded, his voice trembling with emotion, "Yes, Erica. It's me. It's always been me."

He reached out to gently touch her cheek, his fingers trembling. Erica shuddered at his touch and instinctively tried to back away, but her reaction only further infuriated Chris. In a fit of anger, he struck her with the back of his hand, causing her to recoil in pain and fear. Blood oozed from her wounded lip. Chris' anger turned towards himself as he regretted hitting Erica.

In a fit of rage and self-loathing, Chris threw his hands against the glass pane, shattering it into pieces. The shattered glass left cruel, jagged wounds on his skin, the shards digging deep, and causing excruciating pain. With a guttural roar of agony, Chris clutched his injured hand, blood seeping through the gashes as he writhed in torment.

He fell to his knees amidst the shattered glass, his torment mirroring the turmoil that had led him to this desperate act. Amidst the shattered glass and his own anguish, Chris cried out desperately, "Why? Why?" His plea mixed with heartbreaking sobs reverberated through the desolate farmhouse. Erica shuddered at his tormented cries.

With each word, his voice quavered with a potent mixture of sorrow and frustration, as if every syllable carried the weight of years of unspoken affection. "My love for you, Erica," he continued, his words choked with sorrow, "is like shards in the sky. Every time I reach out for your love, I get cut, causing me intolerable pain."

His eyes, once filled with love and longing, were now pools of anguish. He clutched his bleeding hand as if the physical pain could somehow match the emotional torment that had brought him to this point. His voice trembled with a profound sense of longing and despair, echoing the depths of his unrequited love and the torment that had driven him to this dark place.

"This physical pain is nothing compared to my mental agony," he confessed. "You can never be mine." Chris' voice grew more intense as he spoke, his eyes locked onto Erica, who sat bound and terrified in the chair before him. "Now we can only be one in death," he declared with a chilling finality. "Only death can unite us," he continued, his voice taking on a haunting tone.

He had resigned himself to this macabre fate, believing that there was no other way for them to be together. "Let us embrace our love in death," Chris concluded, his voice an ominous whisper that sent a shiver down Erica's spine. As Erica gazed into Chris' eyes, a mixture of fear and pity welled up within her. She could see the torment and anguish that had driven him to this dark place.

But she also knew that she couldn't surrender to his deranged desires. Erica's voice quivered as she spoke, her eyes pleading with Chris to see reason. "Chris," she began softly, "I am sorry for what you had to go through. But I never loved you. I saw you as a good friend. Please, let go of this insanity." Tears welled up in her eyes, reflecting the torment she had endured during her captivity.

She knew that her words held the power to either calm Chris's raging emotions or drive him further into the dark abyss. Chris' expression contorted with a mixture of anguish and disbelief. He had held onto the hope that Erica would reciprocate his feelings. Her rejection was like a dagger through his heart. His grip on his own sanity was slipping as he struggled to process her words.

For a moment, the room hung in an agonizing silence as Chris grappled with the reality of the situation. His love, built on years of longing and obsession, crumbled before him. It was a devastating blow to his fragile psyche. Finally, he spoke, his voice barely above a whisper. "No, Erica, you must be mistaken," he said, his eyes searching hers desperately for a glimmer of affection.

"You will learn to love me. We can make this work. We can make this work in the next dimension. Our souls will be united forever. You and me, Erica. Just you and me". Erica's voice trembled with fear and urgency as she pleaded, "Chris, please, stop this madness at once!" But Chris' emotions had reached a breaking point.

His face contorted into a mix of fury, sadness, and grief as he no longer could bear the weight of Erica's rejection. He grabbed a broken shard from the ground and lunged at her. Time seemed to slow as the shard glinted in the dim light of the room. Erica's heart pounded in her chest as she desperately pushed herself backward, her chair scraping against the floor.

As the shard missed Erica by mere inches, she let out a terrified scream. She closed her eyes tightly. In that moment of sheer dread, a deafening thud echoed through the room causing her to snap her eyes open. To her astonishment, Chris was no longer lunging at her. Instead, he lay motionless on the floor, a pool of crimson spreading from a gunshot wound at the back of his head.

The room was enveloped in an eerie silence, broken only by Erica's own rapid breaths. As she looked ahead, her eyes fell upon a muscular, moustachioed man standing there, a smoking gun still clutched firmly in his hand. Before Erica could fully comprehend what had just occurred, Elena, rushed into the room and enveloped her in a tight embrace.

Tearfully, Elena expressed her gratitude to ACP Wagle, the moustachioed man who had intervened just in the nick of time. ACP Wagle chuckled heartily and quipped, "Well, some policemen do arrive at the right time".Elena's smile was infectious, and it didn't take long for Sophia, Olivia, Amelia, and Isabella to join in the laughter.

Isabella couldn't resist teasing Amelia, saying, "Rush, you tortoise!" Amelia responded with a playful jab, "Hush, you moron!" The Sisterhood's laughter filled the room, creating a sense of camaraderie and warmth that Erica desperately needed. Tears welled up in Erica's eyes as she watched her sister and her friends, the ones who got her out of this nightmare.

Erica did not know whether to laugh or cry, but she felt an overwhelming mix of gratitude and relief. Despite the horrors she had endured, she was now surrounded by the support and love of the Sisterhood. The girls carefully untied the ropes that had bound her. Erica attempted to rise from the chair but found herself too weak and slumped back down.

Elena scolded her gently, "Relax, you dimwit. You're still weak." Erica's face displayed a mixture of shock, relief, and an avalanche of questions. The first question that escaped her lips was, "How? How did you know?" "You'll learn the whole story in due time," Elena chirped. Elena continued, "Sophia played a crucial role in bringing us here and saving you.

But we'll discuss that later. First, we need to get you to a hospital." The priority now was tending to Erica's injuries. Two trained paramedics wheeled in a stretcher and gently transferred Erica onto it. The waiting ambulance would soon transport her to Ashoka Medicover Hospital in Nashik. Elena, Olivia, and Isabella sat in the ambulance as they departed for Nashik.

Amelia and Sophia chose to remain at the farmhouse. Their curiosity was piqued about the enigmatic figure of Roy and what further secrets might be unveiled. Sophia had an inkling that there was a larger puzzle left to be solved. As the investigative team scoured the farmhouse, they stumbled upon a trove of fake documents, all bearing Roy's various aliases.

Passports, Aadhar cards, and a multitude of other identification papers revealed the extent of his deceit and the intricate web of lies he had spun. Each document hinted at a different persona, adding yet another layer of complexity to the mystery surrounding Roy. Among the discoveries in the farmhouse, they also stumbled upon a substantial sum of 50 lakhs in cash.

There was as well an assortment of mobile phones, each equipped

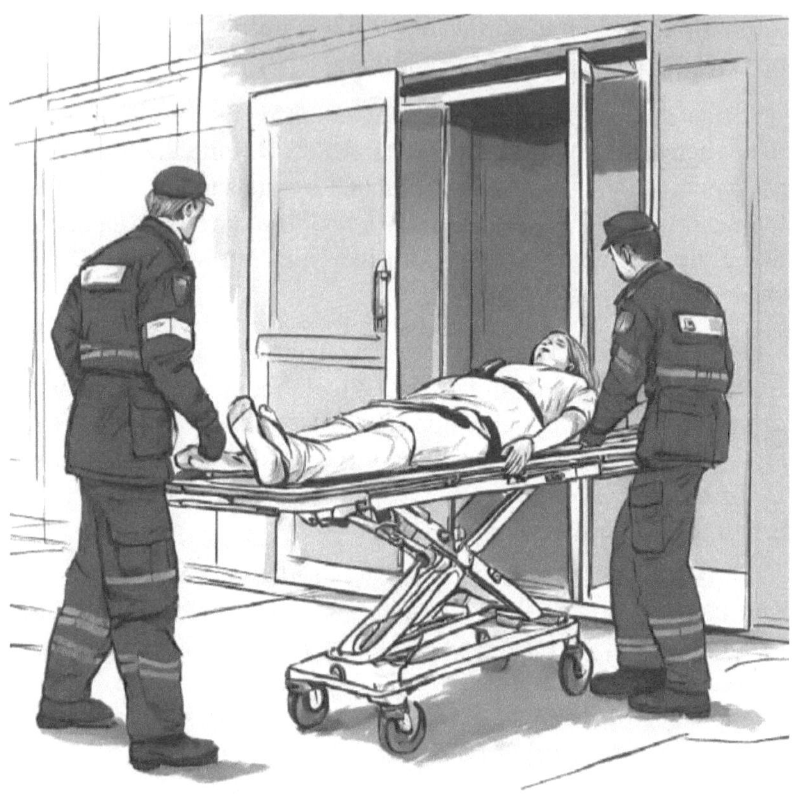

with its own SIM card. Erica had made the shocking revelation about Chris murdering Roy and burying his lifeless body in the backyard. The revelations were piling up, and the mystery was far from over. The team mobilized individuals to begin excavating the hole and retrieve Roy's lifeless body.

In the process, they recovered his shattered mobile phone. ACP Wagle promptly sent it to Simmy for forensic analysis. Additionally, they stumbled upon a keychain with the words 'Demeure Celeste' inscribed on the front and the number '17' on the back. The mysteries of this case continued to unravel, piece by piece.

Chapter 8

Final Triumph or Unfinished Business!

The reunion between Erica and her family was incredibly emotional. Mr. and Mrs. Ramirez held their daughter close, their tears of relief flowing freely. It was a moment that made all the sacrifices and efforts of the Sisterhood feel worthwhile. Mr. Ronald Stevenson and his wife, Mrs. Vinny Stevenson, arrived at the hospital to visit Erica.

They humbly begged for forgiveness for their son Chris' actions and expressed deep shame. In turn, Erica, with a heavy heart, asked forgiveness, acknowledging her unintentional role in Chris' tragic death. ACP Wagle offered his condolence. He expressed regret for the necessity of using force against Chris. Mr. Ramirez, the childhood friend of Ronald, warmly hugged him.

After their visit, Chris' parents bid a tearful farewell. Subsequently, Erica's cousins and family came to visit her, offering support and well-wishes. Juan, Miguel, and Carolina were thrilled with Erica's return. She thanked them profusely for their help in saving her. Uncle Vincent expressed gratitude to the Sisterhood for their relentless determination in locating Erica.

Simmy and Mr. Ranavde visited Erica. Erica hugged Simmy. She expressed her heartfelt thanks for their support in saving her. The group, including Sophia, Amelia, Elena, Olivia, and Isabella, shared a joyous moment, knowing they had accomplished their mission. The relief and joy on Mr. and Mrs. Ramirez's faces was their ultimate reward.

The farmhouse had proven to be a treasure trove of information. Inside, they found evidence that led to the identities of the six girls

Roy had deceived and trafficked earlier. ACP Wagle who got reinstated by Commissioner Deb, took complete charge of the case.

His first mission after getting reinstated was contacting the families of these girls. He shared with them the harrowing truth about how Roy had manipulated their daughters into eloping and then callously sold them into a life of trafficking. It was a difficult conversation to have. The families were overwhelmed with grief, sorrow and anger.

They demanded to know the whereabouts of their missing daughters. ACP Wagle assured them that they would receive answers very soon. He pleaded with the families to keep this information confidential, warning that premature disclosure could alert the criminal syndicate and jeopardize the chances of finding their missing daughters.

ACP Wagle appealed to Commissioner Deb to enforce media silence, emphasizing the need to capture the Kingpin. ACP Wagle arranged the transfer of Roy's phone to Mount Erebus, where Simmy would embark on the task of uncovering the hidden secrets concealed within the device. Simmy delved into the intricate layers of encryption guarding Roy's phone.

It was a formidable digital fortress designed to keep secrets hidden, but Simmy's genius and tenacity were unmatched. Amelia watched in awe as Simmy navigated through virtual mazes, skilfully picking digital locks and bypassing security measures. Minutes turned into hours. And finally, with a triumphant grin, Simmy cracked the last line of defence.

The phone's secrets were now at her fingertips. Inside Roy's encrypted phone, Simmy unearthed a chilling and harrowing array of details concerning the operations and activities of the trafficking syndicate. But there was only one contact saved. It bore a menacing name: 'Maxx Boss.' Simmy read the messages and chat logs with this particular contact.

It sent shivers down Simmy's spine, revealing the disturbing and gruesome nature of their dealings. The conversations revealed a sinister network involved in trafficking girls, with meticulous records of each victim's information. There were discussions about the prices Roy would receive for delivering these innocent souls to an unknown fate.

Dates and details of their impending auctioning at a hidden location were methodically recorded. As the evidence piled up, it became evident that they were dealing with a dangerous and organized criminal trafficking syndicate. As the pieces of the puzzle began to fall into place, it became clear that Roy was just a pawn in the brutal game of female trafficking.

He operated as a mere captain within the organization, following orders from a higher authority. The true kingpin, the mastermind behind this international trafficking ring, remained elusive, pulling the strings from the safety of darkness. ACP Wagle understood that to dismantle this nefarious syndicate and bring the real culprits to justice, they would have to dig deeper.

They would have to uncover the layers of deception and corruption that shielded the true powerbrokers from the law. The fight for justice had just taken a dark and ominous turn. As the gravity of the situation intensified, ACP Wagle called for an emergency meeting at Mount Erebus. Mr. Ranavde and Simmy arrived at the secret headquarters first.

The Sisterhood, accompanied by Miguel, Juan, and Carolina, gathered at Mount Erebus. With a solemn nod, ACP Wagle cleared his throat, addressing the assembled group, "I want to express my sincere gratitude to each one of you for your unwavering determination and relentless efforts in unveiling the secrets behind Erica's disappearance.

Without your collective dedication and personal sacrifices, we wouldn't have made the strides we have in this investigation." The room resounded with a round of heartfelt applause. ACP Wagle acknowledged their support with a nod of appreciation. However, as the applause died down, he continued with a note of caution in his voice.

"Let us not underestimate the adversary we are dealing with. This enemy is exceptionally powerful and exceedingly dangerous. I cannot, in good conscience, risk your lives by involving you in this perilous mission." His words were met with murmurs of dissent from the gathered group. The Sisterhood and their allies were ready to face the challenges head-on regardless of the risks.

ACP Wagle raised his hand to quell the growing unrest, "I understand your determination, and I admire your courage. But our enemy operates in the shadows, and we know very little about their true capabilities. Our priority is to ensure your safety while we pursue this investigation." The room fell into a contemplative silence as the gravity of their situation sank in.

The Sisterhood, Miguel, Juan, Carolina, Mr. Ranavde, and Simmy stepped forward in unison. Elena spoke for the group, "ACP Wagle, we appreciate your concern for our safety, but we want to make it clear that we are willing to fight until the very end. We won't rest until we bring this dangerous kingpin to justice". Mr. Ranavde added his voice to theirs, "We are with them, Wagle Sir.

We share their determination. Together, we will see this through to the end." Simmy chimed in, "Absolutely, we won't back away now. We're all in this together." ACP Wagle saw the fire in their eyes and nodded in acknowledgment. He knew that he couldn't dissuade them from the path they had chosen. ACP Wagle continued, his voice grave and determined.

"Roy, Manek and Rimjhim were just mere foot soldiers in this vast syndicate. While they were dangerous and cunning, our team managed to apprehend them. However, to capture the elusive kingpin behind this operation, we require additional resources and manpower." He glanced around the room."This is not going to be an easy task.

We're dealing with a powerful and shadowy figure who has remained hidden for far too long. Our primary goal is to rescue the missing girls, dismantle the entire operation, and bring this Kingpin to justice. We will convene here shortly to strategize for our upcoming operations. But for now, please take some much-needed rest," ACP Wagle declared.

The Sisterhood soon arrived in Nashik to meet Erica. There was an air of anticipation and curiosity among them. Erica, on the road to recovery was eager to hear the whole story, and she wasn't the only one. Sophia, the one who had led them to the farmhouse was now the centre of attention. All eyes were fixed on her. With an air of anticipation, everyone gathered around Sophia.

Everyone was eager to hear the intricate tale of how she had deduced Chris' involvement and uncovered the location of the farmhouse where Erica had been held captive. She cleared throat and started her explanation, "It all started with the feeling of unease, I couldn't shake off when we arrived for the pre-engagement function".

Sophia continued, "As I observed the dynamics within the family and the atmosphere at the celebration, I noticed a few peculiarities. First and foremost, despite Chris claiming to be Erica's good friend, the way he inconspicuously kept looking at her was far from that of a friend. There was an intensity in his gaze, something more than mere friendship.

His gaze was a complex mix of emotions; love, jealousy, frustration, and anger. But the way he stared at John was different. It radiated pure hatred. It was as if he believed John had stolen something special from him". Sophia continued her explanation, "On the surface, Chris presented himself as Erica's and John's friend. He was even slated to be John's best man.

However, I found this behaviour of Chris extremely peculiar. He was inconsistent in his actions and words," Sophia elaborated. "While he pretended to support Erica's relationship with John, his covert glances and his intense hatred towards John painted a different picture. It was as if he was playing a dual role, concealing his true feelings and intentions.

This behaviour immediately put Chris on my radar". "So, that loud laughter on his funny and not-so-funny jokes were just an act?" "Yes, I just wanted to put him at ease with me", Sophia continued." The day you disappeared, Erica, Chris was not in the hotel for a significant portion of the day. He had arrived late in the evening on that fateful day.

It was indeed peculiar that he would be absent on your wedding day, especially considering that he was originally designated to be John's best man. By the time he arrived, the events had already unfolded. While sharing the events with Chris, I observed something out of the ordinary. His jacket bore unmistakable stains of mud.

Upon closer inspection, I noticed faint, worrisome traces that resembled blood. When I inquired about it, Chris casually explained that he had taken a tumble into a muddy patch. This explanation struck me as odd, especially considering it was the midst of summer, and the monsoon had not yet arrived. Concerned by this, I decided to follow up.

I wanted to check if Chris had taken any steps to clean the jacket. To my surprise, I discovered that he hadn't sent the muddy jacket to the laundry for cleaning. I took it upon myself to investigate further. Sneaking into Chris's room, I combed through his belongings in search of the mysterious jacket. However, my efforts proved fruitless.

There was no sign of the jacket anywhere in his room. It became increasingly evident that Chris had deliberately disposed of the jacket. This was a major red flag for me. Also, during our 'Find Erica' mission, I noticed that Chris would disappear for hours at a stretch. Whenever questioned, he would provide vague excuses, citing personal reasons for his sudden absences.

Little did we know that during those unaccounted hours, he was apparently coming to Kasara to meet and feed you. One day, Chris' car broke down. He seemed extremely anxious and insisted on reaching a certain destination urgently. He left the headquarters and returned very late that day. When he returned, he had another car in his possession, which we later discovered was Roy's car.

In the backseat of that car, I noticed something glimmering. I quietly pocketed the keys from Chris and retrieved the item, which turned out to be Erica's bracelet. To make matters more suspicious, I happened to see Chris disposing something hastily in the waste basket. When I rummaged through the waste basket, I found a torn railway ticket to Kasara.

It immediately reminded me of Rimjhim's mention of Roy's farmhouse in Kasara. The discovery of Erica's bracelet coupled with the Kasara ticket, set off alarm bells in my head. Upon finding these crucial pieces of evidence, I immediately reported it to ACP Wagle. Together, we deduced that Chris had strong connections to the disappearance of both Roy and Erica.

That's when we made the decision to discreetly follow Chris and uncover the truth." Sophia concluded her narrative, "The next day, Chris left for Kasara once again. ACP Wagle followed him, with our team discreetly tagging along. ACP Wagle arrived just in the nick of time. He shot Chris. Erica was saved. And the rest of the story unfolded as you all know."

Erica looked at Sophia with a sense of heartfelt gratitude. Erica hugged Sophia and thanked her. The rest followed suit. "I too thank you for saving Erica's life", boomed a familiar voice. Everyone turned around. It was John. As John approached Erica, the room fell silent. "How are you?", enquired John." "I am doing well. How about you?" , Erica asked weakly.

"I am doing fine", quipped John. Realizing that John and Erica needed space and privacy, the group tactfully made excuses and left, leaving John and Erica alone to process their emotions and reconnect. John gently caressed Erica's hands. Erica's eyes welled with tears. "I am really sorry, John. I wanted to tell you everything, but I just couldn't. Please forgive me".

John's gaze was fixated on the ring adorning Erica's hand, a symbol of their once-blossoming relationship. His voice quivered with a mix of emotions as he asked, "You're still wearing the ring?" And without waiting for a response, he impulsively yanked the ring from her finger. Erica was left stunned and the onlooking group outside the room were in complete shock.

After abruptly yanking the ring from Erica and walking away, John's restless heart couldn't let him leave things unresolved. He turned around and returned to stand before Erica. With determination in his eyes, he went down on one knee and popped the question, "Erica, will you marry me?" The room was filled with a heavy silence.

All eyes were on Erica, awaiting her response to this unexpected twist. Erica, her eyes initially filled with tears of shock were now shedding tears of joy as she exclaimed, "Yes, yes! A thousand times yes!" Laughter filled the room, and smiles abounded as the group, initially stunned by the sudden turn of events rushed in to embrace the once-again newly-engaged couple.

The entire team assembled at Mount Erebus the next day. ACP Wagle turned to the entrance of the room, where a woman with a determined demeanour and a sharp gaze had just entered. He introduced her. "Allow me to introduce you all to Palki Trivedi, the head of our Anti-Trafficking Department. Palki has a wealth of experience in dealing with human trafficking cases.

She's been relentlessly pursuing this syndicate for a long time." Palki Trivedi stood before them, her unwavering gaze locking onto each member of the team, one by one. Her demeanour was resolute, a testament to the years spent in the pursuit of justice. Palki, with her short hair and petite stature, might have appeared unassuming at first glance.

However, her steely gaze and unwavering determination revealed a woman with the courage and tenacity of a tigress. Her sharp mind and years of experience in the field of human trafficking had earned her respect and recognition among her peers. Palki cleared her throat and addressed the group, "Hello, everyone. I am honoured to be a part of this team.

Together, we will dismantle the Kingpin's operation and bring justice to those who have suffered. Let's work tirelessly, shoulder to shoulder, to catch the Kingpin and put an end to this heinous syndicate." Palki, with her extensive experience in anti-trafficking efforts had built a formidable team of specialists dedicated to combating human trafficking.

Among them was Mr. Ramanna, a key figure with a vast network of informers and sources on the ground. Palki introduced him to the gathered team members, emphasizing the importance of his role in their mission. "Meet Mr. Ramanna," Palki said with a nod towards the seasoned informant. "He has a network of informers and sources across the region.

His expertise in gathering critical information has been invaluable in our efforts. Mr. Ranavde and Mr. Ramanna will coordinate closely to ensure we have the most up-to-date and actionable intelligence at our disposal." Palki introduced another key member of their team, Rocko, the cyber specialist with the reputation of an ethical hacker.

Rocko, with his extensive knowledge of the digital realm would

play a crucial role in tracking down the syndicate's activities in the cyber world. "Meet Rocko," Palki said, gesturing towards the cyber expert. "He has a wealth of experience as an ethical hacker. He will be working closely with Simmy to navigate the intricate web of the cyber domain."

Rocko nodded at Simmy and the team. Palki then proceeded to introduce another essential asset they had at their disposal; a dedicated SWAT team. She introduced Mr. Kaur, the head of their SWAT unit. Mr. Kaur's imposing, muscular physique made him appear as solid as a bull. He radiated an aura of strength and resilience that would be vital in executing high-risk operations.

With a cyber specialist team, informers' network, a SWAT team, and the support of the Sisterhood and their allies, ACP Wagle and Palki had assembled an impressive array of resources to confront and dismantle the trafficking syndicate. With a dedicated and well-equipped team, their resolve steeled, and their mission clear, the group was poised and eager to take on the dangerous task ahead.

Chapter 9

The Chase Begins!

The Sisterhood, along with John and Erica were preparing to leave Nashik and return to the Taj Hotel in Mumbai. Erica was finally being discharged from the hospital. Sophia was gazing out of the window, adoring the scenic views passing by. However, amidst the tranquil landscape, something caught her keen eye. "Stop the car" , Sophia yelled.

"Turn the car back. Please, turn the car back," she implored. Without hesitation, John skilfully maneuvered the steering wheel, guiding the car into a precise U-turn. The tires whispered against the asphalt, and the vehicle began retracing their path. "Please stop the car here," Sophia said. Sophia swiftly exited the car and approached the gate, where a sign read, 'Demeure Celeste'.

The name on the gate matched the one on the keychain she had found earlier. Realization washed over her. Without hesitation, she reached for her phone and dialled ACP Wagle's number, her heart racing with anticipation. As ACP Wagle and Palki Trivedi received the call from Sophia, they acted swiftly. The Sisterhood, John and Erica awaited them with bated breath.

Accompanied by Mr. Ranavde, Mr. Ramanna, Mr. Kaur, and the SWAT team, ACP Wagle and Palki Trivedi rushed to the location marked 'Demeure Celeste'. This was no ordinary place. It was a gated community. The keychain's number, '17', matched the villa's number at Demeure Celeste. ACP Wagle displayed his identification to the security personnel.

They immediately allowed them entry into the exclusive community. As they approached Villa No. 17, they were met with a

sight of opulence and luxury. This magnificent villa stood as a testament to wealth and extravagance. Its sprawling grounds and grandeur left no doubt that something significant was concealed within these lavish walls.

Inside Villa No. 17 at Demeure Celeste, opulence and luxury extended to every corner. The expansive foyer greeted them with a dazzling crystal chandelier hanging from the ceiling, casting a soft, warm glow across the marble floors. The walls were adorned with priceless artwork. Intricate Persian rugs covered the floors. As they ventured further, they entered a spacious living room.

Plush, velvet-upholstered sofas and armchairs were arranged around a massive, intricately designed coffee table. The room was adorned with more exquisite art pieces and sculptures. Floor-to-ceiling windows offered a breath-taking view of a well-manicured garden, complete with a sparkling swimming pool. The dining area featured a grand, polished mahogany table.

Crystal glassware, fine chinaware, and silverware were carefully arranged on the table. A fully equipped modern kitchen sat adjacent, with state-of-the-art appliances and gleaming granite counter tops. Moving upstairs, they discovered a luxurious master bedroom. A massive four-poster bed dominated the room, draped in luxurious silk sheets.

The ensuite bathroom boasted a jacuzzi, a walk-in shower, and marble fixtures.The villa seemed to have numerous rooms each reflecting a level of opulence that only the wealthiest could afford. Every detail, from the ornate light fixtures to the meticulously designed furniture oozed extravagance. However, the team found the villa seemingly deserted.

ACP Wagle's experience told him that something was amiss. He called for additional manpower to ensure a thorough search of the premises. The extra personnel arrived swiftly. Together, they embarked on a systematic exploration of the villa, room by room, corner by corner. Every nook and cranny were carefully examined, but the villa gave away no secrets.

There were no signs of forced entry or struggle. The rooms remained undisturbed, as though frozen in time. Sophia's keen eye for detail didn't disappoint as she continued her exploration of Villa No. 17 at Demeure Celeste. While in the lavish master bedroom, she noticed a subtle irregularity in the pattern of the wallpaper. She chose to investigate further.

Upon closer inspection, she realized that one section of the wall felt slightly hollow when she pressed against it. A soft click followed as the wallpaper concealed a hidden door.With cautious excitement, Sophia pushed the concealed door, revealing a secret chamber behind it. The hidden room was small but packed with treasures. Stacks of cash were neatly arranged on shelves.

Sophia couldn't help but be awestruck by the sheer amount of money before her. But that wasn't all. The room held even more secrets. There were stacks of gold coins, glittering like a pirate's treasure trove. Sophia's heart raced as she realized the extent of the wealth hidden away in this secret chamber. The team's collective gasp echoed through the room as they stepped inside.

Alongside the precious metals and cash, they discovered a collection of forged documents: passports, driver's licenses, and IDs; all bearing different names and disguises. The IDs seemed to confirm what they had suspected; this luxurious villa was a hub for illegal activities, possibly linked to human trafficking. The hidden room was filled with money, gold coins, and falsified identification.

It was a treasure trove of evidence that could help them expose the criminals behind this operation. It seemed as though the place had been abandoned in a hurry leaving behind the hidden treasure and documents as the only evidence of illicit activities. Among the documents in the hidden room, Amelia found an envelope with a handwritten note addressed to someone named 'Maxx Boss'.

The note contained cryptic references to the recent events and hinted at a sense of urgency.Whoever had been operating from this villa had fled hastily leaving behind valuable evidence.With the evidence in hand, ACP Wagle knew that they needed to act swiftly. The team gathered the money, gold coins, IDs, and any relevant documents, sealing them as potential evidence.

Their next step would be to analyse the findings, connect the dots, and determine the links between this hidden chamber, the trafficking syndicate, and the mysterious 'Maxx Boss'. The focus of the investigation shifted to deciphering the whereabouts of Maxx Boss, the elusive Kingpin who had orchestrated the trafficking syndicate.

Simmy and Rocko delved deeper into the digital realm to uncover any digital footprints left behind by Maxx Boss. They meticulously traced communication channels, encrypted messages, and online activities that might lead to valuable insights about this mysterious figure. On the other hand, Mr. Ranavde and Mr. Ramanna leveraged their extensive network of informers.

They combed through their sources, seeking any morsel of information related to Maxx Boss. These informers, operating in the shadows, had proven their worth in previous investigations. And now they were tasked with unearthing the secrets surrounding this enigmatic individual. The breakthrough they had been waiting for finally arrived.

The informers provided a crucial name - 'Maxx Nickolav'. Armed with this information, Simmy and Rocko sprang into action. They embarked on an intricate digital hunt, tracking Maxx Nickolav through the labyrinthine web of the digital realm.The ease with which they found Maxx Nickolav's digital footprint raised suspicions among the team.

They couldn't help but wonder whether this was the real Maxx Boss or a clever decoy designed to mislead them. Maxx Nickolav's presence on social media platforms like Facebook and Instagram seemed almost too convenient. It left them with nagging doubts. Upon closer inspection, Maxx Nickolav's online profiles were filled with an array of photos showcasing a lavish lifestyle.

These images featured him surrounded by beautiful women, posing at exotic locations, and indulging in extravagant parties. While this might have seemed like a convincing portrayal of a wealthy and influential individual, Simmy and Rocko knew better than to take things at face value. The digital trail was far from straightforward.

As they continued to dig deeper into Maxx Nickolav's online presence, they hoped to uncover the truth behind this enigmatic figure. They knew that beneath the veneer of luxury and indulgence, there might be crucial clues that would lead them closer to unravelling the secrets of the criminal syndicate and its elusive Kingpin.

As Simmy and Rocko continued to analyse Maxx Nickolav's social media profiles, they chanced upon a crucial lead. Among the many lavish photos depicting his opulent lifestyle, there was one that held the key they had been desperately searching for. In this particular image, Maxx Nickolav was holding a key with the unmistakable emblem of Demeure Celeste.

Although this detail was not immediately visible to the naked eye, Simmy and Rocko were not ordinary investigators. Armed with sophisticated software and cutting-edge methods, they set to work enhancing the image. After meticulous scrutiny, they made a definitive confirmation: Maxx Nickolav was indeed the elusive Maxx Boss, the mastermind behind the criminal syndicate.

Maxx Nickolav's overconfidence had led him to flaunt this vital clue, believing that no one could ever decipher his true identity. However, he had underestimated the relentless determination and advanced skills of Simmy and Rocko, who had now pierced through the facade he had so carefully constructed. Simmy and Rocko made a crucial breakthrough.

The team was one step closer to uncovering the full extent of Maxx Boss's operations and dismantling the criminal empire that had eluded them for so long. Upon confirming Maxx Nickolav's true identity, ACP Wagle swiftly issued an amber alert for him. As ACP Wagle and his team raced against time to close in on Maxx Nickolav, they were astonished by his audacious move.

Despite being on the radar of law enforcement, Maxx Nickolav's unwavering confidence led him to book a plane ticket to Mumbai using his real name. Despite the lack of concrete proof linking the two identities, they believed their plan would lay the trap to catch the Kingpin. They meticulously crafted a plan to ensnare Maxx Nickolav A.K.A., Maxx Boss.

While the law enforcement team was cautious not to underestimate the dangerous Maxx Boss, they couldn't help but feel that the climax of their long pursuit was drawing near, and that the final confrontation might be within their grasp. The flight from Bahamas to Mumbai touched down. Maxx Nickolav, flanked by his two imposing bodyguards began to disembark.

As they traversed the airport, a group of CRPF guards swiftly closed in around them. Maxx was swiftly escorted to a secure room. His bodyguards were escorted to a separate room. Maxx Nickolav's fierce demeanour intensified. He unleashed a barrage of abuse and screams at the guards clearly agitated by the unexpected turn of events.

Inside the secure room, Maxx Nickolav's mobile phones were confiscated leaving him without his usual means of communication and control. As the tension in the secure room escalated, a senior official named Mr. Kumar entered and addressed Maxx Nickolav. In a stern and authoritative tone, he stated, "Mr. Maxx Tickolav, you have been placed under arrest."

Maxx, in a fit of anger and frustration, retorted, "I am not Maxx Tickolav, you moron. I am Maxx Nickolav. Release me immediately, or be prepared to face the consequences. "Unfazed by Maxx's prot ests or threats, Mr. Kumar ordered one of the guards to produce Maxx Nickolav's passport. When the passport was presented, it displayed the name 'Maxx Nickolav' on it.

Mr. Kumar, recognizing the grave misunderstanding offered a profuse apology to Maxx."We are deeply sorry, Mr.Nickolav," he said sincerely."It seems there was a mix-up between you and another individual, Mr. Maxx Tickolav. We deeply regret any inconvenience this may have caused you. Please accept our apologies. You are free to leave."

Where are my phones?", Maxx thundered. In response, Mr. Kumar swiftly issued an order to the guard , instructing him to retrieve Maxx's phones without delay. As the guard returned with the phones, Mr .Kumar personally handed them over to Maxx, who eagerly snatched them back. Mr. Kumar stated, "I deeply apologize for the inconvenience you've experienced, Mr. Nickolav.

We regret any anxiety this has caused you. Please know that we are taking measures to prevent such occurrences in the future. Maxx was furious. He threatened to get all of them sacked. "You have no idea who I am," he grow led in his menacing Russian accent, his eyes blazing with fury. "I know Mr. Putin personally. You will most certainly hear from him about this."

"In a fit of fury, Maxx, flanked by his two formidable Russian bodyguards, stormed out of the room. They exited the premises in a solemn procession. Maxx swiftly climbed into a waiting Prado, ready to depart in haste. Maxx's fury began to subside. As he reflected on the situation, his anger turned into amusement. He couldn't deny it was an honest mistake.

As he remembered the faces of the guards, who were begging for forgiveness, and the somewhat comical sight of the official profusely apologizing before him, Maxx couldn't help but crack a smile. A hearty guffaw escaped Maxx's lips, and he couldn't contain his amusement. Little did Maxx know; the entire scenario had been meticulously orchestrated as an elaborate ruse.

While Maxx had been caught up in the drama surrounding the mistaken identity and the subsequent apologies, Mr. Kumar's team had a covert agenda. Their true aim was to gain access to Maxx's mobile phones. As soon as Maxx's phones were confiscated, Simmy and Rocko took over and, assumed their roles with the utmost precision and discretion.

They immediately set to work, their nimble fingers deftly installing a highly sophisticated and hidden spyware on the phones.This spyware was designed to operate in the shadows, completely undetectable to the untrained eye. It would provide the team with access to Maxx's communications, contacts, and even his GPS location, all without his knowledge.

Maxx's phones, as it turned out, were not your average devices. They were equipped with top-tier encryption. This presented a formidable challenge for Simmy and Rocko, but their expertise was matched only by their determination. While it wasn't possible to access all the information in a matter of minutes, they had succeeded in stealthily installing the spyware.

With the spyware in place, the team now had a subtle but powerful advantage. They could tap into Maxx's conversations, gaining insight into his plans, connections, and communication. They could track his movements in real-time. Additionally, they could monitor his chats, providing them with a window into his digital interactions.

While Maxx believed the apologies had put an end to the matter, a covert operation was now underway. The team was ready to delve into the depths of Maxx's digital life, all under the guise of a simple mix-up. Little did Maxx suspect the web of intrigue that had just been woven around him.A group of vehicles covertly tailed Maxx's car maintaining a discreet distance.

Among these vehicles was Simmy and Rocko's mobile cybervan, a veritable fortress of high-tech surveillance equipment. The Sisterhood joined forces with them. The Sisterhood, Simmy and Rocko were huddled together. Their eyes were glued on to the array of monitors displaying live feeds and data streams.They had successfully infiltrated Maxx's phones.

But they encountered a formidable obstacle: a maze of numbers arranged haphazardly, a testament to the encryption's complexity. Cracking this encryption proved to be a formidable challenge, one that required time, skill, and precision. Each passing moment added to the suspense as they inched closer to unlocking the treasure trove of information contained within Maxx's devices.

Chapter 10

The Kingpin Unveiled?

As Maxx Nickolav's phone rang, the tension inside the cybervan reached its peak. Maxx answered the phone.

Maxx: *Da zdravstvuyet Koroleva Nikolava!*

An unexpected shrill, female voice from the other side of the call sent shivers down Maxx Nickolav's spine.

Unknown Female: *K chertu vashi pozdravleniya!*

Durak, tvoye prikrytiye raskryto.

YA preduprezhdal tebya o tvoyey samouverennosti.

Vasha samouverennost' dorogo nam oboshlas'.

Adskiy ogon', durak. Adskiy ogon', durak!

Maxx Nickolav: *Adskiy ogon', Mat'.*

Izvini. Adskiy ogon', Koroleva Nikolave.

The line went dead.

Maxx wasted no time in reacting to the alarming phone call. With adrenaline surging, he ordered his Prado to accelerate at full throttle. His Russian bodyguards sprang into action, firing warning shots into the air in rapid succession. The deafening gunshots reverberated through the surroundings, sending shockwaves of panic through the drivers of the vehicles trailing Maxx's Prado.

In their frenzied attempts to escape the gunfire, several of the trailing vehicles swerved and collided with one another, creating a chaotic blockade on the road. The cacophony of screeching tires and crunching metal further fuelled the pandemonium, effectively preventing the tailing vehicles from pursuing the speeding Prado. The situation was a complete disaster.

Maxx's quick thinking and the sheer intimidation factor of his bodyguards had disrupted the pursuit and bought him a temporary reprieve. Inside the cybervan, the team watched in astonishment as their meticulously planned operation unravelled in a matter of seconds. They were utterly astounded by the rapid sequence of events that unfolded before them.

Inside the cybervan, the team recognized that the key to understanding Maxx's sudden change in behaviour lay in deciphering the contents of that mysterious phone call. Time was of the essence, and they needed to generate a transcript as quickly as possible. With practiced efficiency, they extracted the recording of the phone call.

They fed it into their state-of-the-art translation software. The high-end software worked its magic, rapidly analysing the audio and converting it into a coherent transcript. As the seconds ticked by, tension gripped the van's occupants. Finally, the transcript was ready, and they eagerly scanned the text, hoping to uncover the information that had triggered Maxx's reaction.

Maxx: *Da zdravstvuyet Koroleva Nikolave!*

Long Live, Queen Nickolav!

Unknown Female:*K chertu vashi pozdravleniya!*

Damn your greetings!

Durak, tvoye prikrytiye raskryto.

Fool, your cover is blown!

YA preduprezhdal tebya o tvoyey samouverennosti.

I warned you about your overconfidence!

Vasha samouverennost' dorogo nam oboshlas'.

Your overconfidence has cost us dearly!

Adskiy ogon', durak.

Hellfire, fool!

Adskiy ogon', durak.

HELLFIRE, Fool!

Maxx: *Adskiy ogon', Mat'.*
Hellfire, Mother.
Izvini.
Sorry!
Adskiy ogon', Koroleva Nikolave.
Hellfire, Queen Nickolav!

The shared transcript within the team brought forth revelations that flabbergasted the team. It shattered their assumptions and turned the operation on its head. It was now clear that Maxx Nickolav wasn't the elusive "Kingpin" they had been pursuing. Instead, the true power behind the scenes was a Queenpin; Queen Nickolav, Maxx's mother.

The transcript unveiled a startling truth: Maxx Nickolav was not the mastermind, but rather a key figure executing the orders. He played the role of a general, carrying out the commands and wishes of Queen Nickolav, the enigmatic Queenpin who had eluded their attention until now. The team had been chasing the wrong target. The dynamics of their operation had shifted dramatically.

The Queenpin was the true focus, and Maxx Nickolav's actions were under her influence. The unfolding revelations continued to stun the team. Not only did Queen Nickolav know that Maxx's cover had been blown, but she had also issued a chilling command in response to the threat they posed. In the transcript, her ominous directive was clear.

Maxx was to burn everything to the ground, leaving no trace of evidence behind. ACP Wagle recognized that the Prado, which now held Maxx Nickolav, was on a potentially dangerous path. It had to be stopped at all costs. With determination and resolve, ACP Wagle issued an amber alert for the Prado, mobilizing all available resources.

The order was clear; the Prado had to be intercepted and brought to a halt, no matter the consequences. Police stations along the suspected route of the Prado were put on high alert, preparing for a possible firefight. Officers and units were deployed strategically, bracing themselves for the imminent confrontation.

Maxx Nickolav, realizing the impending danger, activated the self-destruct mode on all his phones and hurled them out of the speeding Prado. Panic set inside the cybervan. Simmy and Rocko, now faced an impossible challenge. They had just one minute to extract all the crucial information from the devices before they were destroyed.

As the seconds ticked away, the tension in the van grew multifold. Time seemed to both stretch and compress simultaneously, weaving

a surreal and intense atmosphere. Every passing moment counted. The pressure to retrieve the data mounted with each heartbeat, the weight of their mission pressing down on them.

Simmy and Rocko worked with frantic intensity, their fingers dancing over the keyboards as they attempted to breach the phones' defences and salvage the critical information. The countdown to destruction felt like an eternity. Yet it was slipping through their grasp like sand in an hourglass. Beads of sweat formed on their foreheads, mingling with the weight of the ticking clock.

The countdown from 10 began, each second feeling like an eternity in the cybervan.

'**10...**' "Time is running out," ACP Wagle's voice crackled.

'**9...**' "Come on, Simmy." "Rocko, hurry!"

'**8...**' The downloading bar on their screens seemed to be lagging painfully behind the relentless self-destruct countdown.

'**7...**' "Guys, we have just seconds left."

'**6...**' Rivulets of sweat trickled down everyone's faces.

'**5...**' Heartbeats drummed in a frantic rhythm.

'**4...**' "Rocko, Simmy, you can do it!"

'**3...**' The downloading bar still struggling to catch up.

'**2...**' Time seemed to freeze, as if the universe itself held its breath.

'**1...**' Just one second remained, a nail-biting climax.

A piercing, loud beep shattered the silence, leaving everyone shocked to the core. An overwhelming sense of suspense and dread hung in the air, thickening the tension.

"Download complete," announced the robotic AI voice, signalling the completion of the download.

'**0...**' The phones went into self-destruct mode, disintegrating into a cloud of fragments, leaving behind only traces of their digital existence.

The team in the cybervan heaved a collective sigh of relief. They all gathered in a collective huddle. They had narrowly averted disaster, snatching the vital information from the jaws of destruction in the final, heart-pounding seconds. As the dust settled, the van's occupants knew they had won a crucial battle in this high-stakes game, but the war was far from over.

Sophia's relieved words, "Whew, that was close," hung in the air for only a fleeting moment before a startling news report sent shockwaves through the communication lines. The Prado carrying Maxx Nickolav had been brought to a sudden stop, pinned down at a chaotic intersection. The law enforcement officers encircled the van and ordered the occupants to surrender.

On that fateful crossroad, a fierce exchange of gunfire erupted between the Prado's occupants and the law enforcement officers. The deafening noise of heavy firepower echoed through the streets as both sides fiercely fought for supremacy. However, the odds were overwhelmingly against the Prado's passengers. Despite their valiant efforts, Maxx's bodyguards were heavily outgunned.

They faced insurmountable odds. The Prado eventually fell silent, and a tense stillness settled over the intersection. When the officers cautiously approached the scene, they discovered the lifeless bodies of Maxx's loyal bodyguards, a sombre testament to their dedication and sacrifice. But Maxx Nickolav had managed to slip away leaving no trace behind.

His escape was nothing short of a Houdini act, as if he had dissolved into thin air. The pursuit had taken yet another unexpected turn. Maxx had eluded their grasp, leaving the team to grapple with the reality that their quarry had once again vanished into the shadows. With Maxx's elusive escape leaving them with few leads, the team was left with only one viable option.

They had to quickly decipher the encrypted numbers from the phones they had managed to salvage before destruction. Inside the cybervan, the atmosphere was tense yet resolute. The two hackers worked feverishly on decrypting the mysterious numbers, their fingers flying over keyboards as lines of code filled their screens. Every passing second was precious.

As they delved deeper into the encryption, it felt like a digital chess match against an unseen adversary. The encrypted numbers were a puzzle, a labyrinth of information that needed to be unravelled. The team's hopes hinged on what they would discover once they cracked this digital enigma. Simmy and Rocko's efforts were relentless.

They were determined to expose the truth, no matter how well hidden it might be. In the dimly-lit room, Simmy and Rocko huddled over their screens. Their eyes were locked onto a seemingly inscrutable sequence of numbers they had spent hours trying to decipher. Frustration had given way to determination. And at long last, a breakthrough had occurred.

They had successfully decoded the enigma before them. Their jubilation was short-lived, however. The numbers they had unveiled appeared to be random and meaningless. It provided no immediate insight into their significance. It was then that Amelia, a cryptography expert among their team stepped forward to tackle the puzzle.

Amelia's expertise in deciphering codes and ciphers was legendary, and she approached the challenge with unwavering confidence. As she meticulously examined the sequence, patterns began to emerge from the seemingly chaotic digits. With each moment, her understanding grew clearer until it struck her like a bolt of lightning.

These numbers were not arbitrary. They formed the coordinates of a specific location. As the realization dawned on her, Amelia felt a surge of excitement mixed with trepidation. She quickly cross-referenced the numbers on the mapping software. As the team gazed at the digital map, the coordinates they had deciphered pointed unerringly to a specific location: Vanakbara Beach in Silvassa.

The revelation struck them like a thunderbolt as it became unmistakably clear that this was not just any place. It was the epicentre of the syndicate's operations, the very heart of their clandestine dealings. Silvassa, around 166 kilometres from Mumbai was known for its pristine beaches, serene landscapes and calm atmosphere. It seemed an unlikely hub for such covert activities.

Yet, here lay the bidding centre and the main headquarters of Queen Nickolav's syndicate, hidden in plain sight amidst the tranquil beauty of Vanakbara Beach. It was at this very location that Queen Nickolav had ordered Maxx to carry out his mission of destruction that now held chilling implications for the team. Rocko wasted no time in sending the coordinates to everyone.

This sparked a flurry of discussions and preparations within the team. The countdown had begun. The team was ready to descend upon the beach, fully aware that the impending confrontation could be their most perilous yet. In response to the critical information provided by Rocko, ACP Wagle and Palki Trivedi understood the urgency of the situation at Vanakbara Beach.

They swiftly assembled a large and highly trained tactical team, armed with an array of formidable weaponry to ensure they were prepared for any potential threat. Palki contacted the state armoury in Thane and requested weapons suitable for an operation of this magnitude and significance. They selected the most formidable weapons available from the armoury.

Assault rifles like the M4 Carbine and AK-47 for close-quarter combat. Sniper Rifles with precision optics such as the Remington 700 and the Barrett M82 that allowed for long-range accuracy, essential for spotting and eliminating threats from a distance. Shotguns like the Benelli M4 and Mossberg 590 for close encounters and breaching doors if necessary.

Belt-fed machine guns, like the M249 SAW and PKM that offered sustained automatic fire. Pistols, typically semi-automatic handguns such as Glock 17 and Sig Sauer P226 that served as secondary weapons for each team member. Fragmentation grenades for clearing rooms and disabling threats within enclosed spaces, smoke grenades for concealment.

The team donned heavy body armour vests and helmets, providing protection against ballistic threats. Tactical gear such as night-vision goggles, flashlights, and communication equipment ensured the team's effectiveness in low-light conditions and facilitated coordination. First aid kits and trauma gear were carried to treat injuries promptly during the operation.

Breaching Tools like battering rams, bolt cutters, and breaching charges allowed the team to gain access to secured areas if needed. Surveillance drones equipped with cameras and thermal imaging capabilities that provided valuable situational awareness. They were now fully prepared for the final battle. The tactical teams wasted no time as they swiftly settled into their armoured vans.

Each van carried a carefully assembled team consisting of one commander, a vice commander, and eight highly trained KOBRA commandos. KOBRA or Knights of Battlefield Reconnaissance and Assault were one of the most highly-trained commandos in the world. The commandos equipped with a formidable array of weaponry and gear were ready for the mission ahead.

The convoy of ten armoured vans embarked on the high-speed journey towards Silvassa, their vehicles designed to provide both protection and mobility in potentially dangerous situations. Inside each van, the team members double-checked their equipment and maintained a focused demeanour, prepared for whatever challenges awaited them at Vanakbara Beach.

Following closely behind, Mr. Kaur and his SWAT team, known for their exceptional skills in close-quarter combat, ensured that they were ready to provide support as needed. Their presence added an extra layer of expertise to the operation. Meanwhile, ACP Wagle and Palki Trivedi, both seasoned law enforcement professionals, donned their protective vests and joined the convoy.

Their leadership and experience were invaluable as they prepared to lead the operation to confront Queen Nickolav and dismantle her sinister syndicate. Commissioner Deb observed from his headquarters, keeping a keen eye on the operation. The armoured convoy raced towards its destination followed closely by ACP Wagle and Palki Trivedi.

The cybervan expertly maintained a safe distance, strategically positioned to carry out crucial reconnaissance activities. Their role was pivotal, as they were entrusted with providing invaluable intelligence and maintaining a covert presence. Within the cybervan, the team's expertise in cyber warfare and surveillance would come to the forefront.

They deployed cutting-edge drones equipped with advanced cameras and sensors, allowing them to discreetly survey the area from the skies. These drones were capable of capturing high-resolution imagery, conducting thermal scans, and relaying real-time data back to the team. ACP Wagle and Palki Trivedi were issuing orders.

In recognition of the dedication and sacrifices of the Sisterhood, Simmy, Palki Trivedi, SI Srilakshmi, Erica, and the countless girls ensnared by the female trafficking syndicate, ACP Wagle aptly codenamed the operation "Operation Devi Shakti." This name paid tribute to the divine feminine power and represented the courage and strength of all those involved in the battle against the syndicate.

The armoured convoy arrived at Vanakbara Beach. ACP Wagle, Palki Trivedi, and the cybervan arrived behind them. The teams swiftly assumed their positions. A tense hush fell over the area as everyone awaited the command from ACP Wagle. ACP Wagle declared, "Let Operation Devi Shakti proceed." Operation Devi Shakti was on.

The cyber team wasted no time in deploying their arsenal of specialized drones to survey the area. Their collection of drones was nothing short of impressive, each designed to serve a distinct purpose and provide critical information. Hummingbird drones were nimble, fast-flying drones darted through the air like their namesake birds.

They quickly captured essential information and relayed it to the team in real-time. Their agility and speed made them ideal for rapid reconnaissance. Insect Drones were tiny, inconspicuous drones that were masters of camouflage and subtlety.

They blended seamlessly into the environment allowing them to discreetly monitor ongoing activities.

The insect drones provided a constant loop of invaluable data. Vulture drones among the most formidable in their arsenal were equipped with offensive capabilities. These versatile machines were capable of firing bullets and launching grenades. They offered a powerful deterrent against potential threats allowing the team to maintain control of the situation.

With this diverse fleet of drones at their disposal, the cyber team was able to conduct comprehensive surveillance of Vanakbara Beach from every angle. The Hummingbird drones provided rapid updates. The Insect drones kept a constant watch. The Vulture drones stood ready to respond to any emerging threats. Their synchronized efforts created a digital web of intelligence.

This ensured that the team had eyes on every corner of the beach, ready to relay crucial information to the tactical teams on the ground. The tactical team advanced to the ruins of Mogardo Fort. The adversaries remained concealed within, lurking in the fortress's shadows. The tactical team and the SWAT team encircled the fort's ruins.

The dilapidated Mogardo Fort ruins, at first glance, appeared as nothing more than a relic of a bygone era, seemingly inconspicuous in the tranquil surroundings of Vanakbara Beach. However, what lay beneath the surface was a stark contrast to its weathered exterior. The syndicate had ingeniously transformed the fort into an impenetrable underground fortress.

Beneath the fort's crumbling facades, cutting-edge technology thrived in secrecy. The syndicate had spared no expense in outfitting their underground lair with state-of-the-art equipment and defenses. Surveillance cameras, biometric security systems, and encrypted communication networks were just a few of the technological marvels that safeguarded their secrets.

Formidable weapons were strategically stockpiled, ensuring the fortress's capability to repel any intrusion. Armouries housed an array of advanced firearms. And fortified positions were designed to hold their ground against potential threats. The syndicate had constructed their underground haven to withstand even the most determined assaults.

In the skies above, the syndicate had deployed its own squadron of drones, a testament to their commitment to maintaining an upper hand in the digital and aerial realms. These drones were equipped with advanced sensors, capable of both surveillance and defence. They patrolled the airspace, providing an additional layer of security and surveillance.

The KOBRA teams' entry in the underground fortress beneath the Mogardo Fort ruins set the stage for an epic confrontation between the KOBRA teams and the formidable Syndicate force. As the two forces clashed, it was clear that despite being outnumbered, the KOBRA teams held a significant advantage in terms of training, coordination, and cutting-edge technology.

The battle commenced with an air of tension and anticipation. The KOBRA teams under the command of their skilled commanders moved with precision and stealth through the darkened corridors of the underground fortress. The Syndicate mafia, a mix of nationalities were determined but faced a daunting challenge. KOBRA's tactical mastery was evident.

They advanced utilizing the fortress's layout to their advantage. Their movements were coordinated and synchronized, demonstrating their unwavering discipline and training. The diverse composition of the KOBRA teams, representing various Indian regions enabled them to bring a wide range of skills to bear. Their teamwork was seamless.

KOBRA's technological advantage, including advanced drones for surveillance and reconnaissance gave them a critical upper hand. They could identify enemy positions, traps, and ambushes. The battle erupted into fierce firefights as both sides exchanged rounds of ammunition.KOBRA's precise marksmanship and advanced weaponry gave them the upper hand.

The Syndicate force was pushed into a defensive posture. Amidst the chaos, several KOBRA team members made heroic sacrifices to protect their comrades. KOBRA executed a brilliantly devised ambush that caught the Syndicate mafia off-guard. The surprise attack inflicted heavy casualties on the opposition, leaving them disoriented and struggling to regroup.

With casualties mounting, their cohesion started to erode. The syndicate attempted to retreat, but were relentlessly pursued by KOBRA. In the end, the Syndicate forces suffered heavy losses and were annihilated. KOBRA emerged victorious, but not without their own share of casualties. The hard-fought battle had taken its toll, and they mourned the loss of their comrades.

In the depths of the underground fortress, a high-stakes battle of drones erupted. The Vulture drones clashed with the Syndicate's fleet of drones. As the Vulture drones charged into the fortress, they were met with the Syndicate's drones, each equipped with its own set of advanced capabilities. The Vulture drones had the capacity to fire bullets and launch grenades.

The Syndicate's drones, on the other hand, possessed stealth and agility as their primary advantages. They moved with the grace of birds, evading incoming fire and attempting to outmanoeuvre the Vulture drones. The battle unfolded as a complex game of cat and mouse. The Vulture drones sought to lock onto their elusive targets in the air.

The Syndicate's drones weaved through the underground caverns, attempting to stay out of harm's way. The Vulture drones unleashed precision strikes, sending bullets and grenades hurtling toward their Syndicate counterparts. Explosions echoed through the fortress as the two sides exchanged fire, the thunderous sounds reverberating through the underground passages.

The Syndicate's drones performed evasive manoeuvres to avoid the onslaught of gunfire. They darted behind cover and utilized the fortress's architecture to shield themselves from the continuous barrage of firing. Amidst the chaos, a decisive moment arrived. One of the Vulture drones managed to lock onto a Syndicate drone, firing a well-aimed burst of bullets.

The Syndicate's drone spiralled out of control, crashing into the fortress walls in a fiery explosion. With the loss of their drones mounting, the Syndicate's aerial force faced inevitable defeat. Finally, the last remnants of the Syndicate's drone fleet were eliminated. The Vulture drones continued to patrol the skies maintaining aerial dominance over the underground fortress.

With the aerial battle of drones concluded, Mr. Kaur and his elite SWAT team entered the underground fortress through a concealed opening, determined to confront the remaining syndicate henchmen. Moving with practiced stealth, Mr. Kaur and his SWAT team advanced deeper into the labyrinthine corridors of the underground fortress.

The SWAT team soon encountered a group of syndicate henchmen guarding a crucial junction. In the dim light, the henchmen's faces were twisted with determination as they readied themselves for a fight. With a resounding battle cry, Mr. Kaur and his team charged toward the henchmen. A fierce hand-to-hand combat ensued.

The narrow passageway became a battleground, echoing with the sounds of grunts, blows, and gunfire. The SWAT team's impeccable training and coordination became evident as they fought valiantly to eliminate their adversaries. Mr. Kaur displayed his exceptional leadership and combat skills, guiding his team with tactical precision.

They utilized the environment to their advantage, using cover and ambush tactics to gain the upper hand. As the battle raged on, the SWAT team's overwhelming force began to wear down the remaining syndicate henchmen. In the midst of the chaos, a critical moment arrived. Mr. Kaur, leading by example, engaged in a fierce one-on-one battle with one of the syndicate's henchmen.

Despite his remarkable skills, he met a formidable adversary. In a heroic act of self-sacrifice, Mr. Kaur managed to subdue his opponent but suffered fatal injuries in the process. Mr. Kaur's sacrifice fueled the anger within the SWAT team, driving them to launch an aggressive assault on the remaining henchmen with the fury of the Gods.

With Mr. Kaur's final act, the remaining syndicate henchmen were overwhelmed by the SWAT team's superior firepower and unwavering determination. The corridor fell silent, save for the heavy breaths of the SWAT team, who had emerged victorious. As the SWAT team regrouped, they paid their respects to Mr. Kaur, the only casualty in the intense hand-to-hand combat.

With the three decisive battles behind them, the KOBRA commandos, the SWAT team, and ACP Wagle and Palki Trivedi ventured deeper into the heart of the underground fortress. Following closely behind were the Sisterhood, Simmy, and Rocko. As they entered the main cavern, their senses were immediately overwhelmed by the shocking sight that greeted them.

The sheer enormity of the underground chamber took their breath away. But what truly stunned them was the unexpected marvel above; a painted ceiling, awash in a brilliant shade of blue. The team's shock intensified as they laid eyes on an utterly horrifying spectacle. Words alone fell short in capturing the unfolding spectacle before them.

Suspended from the cavern's vast expanse were hundreds of glistening cages, each containing young girls and women who were barely clothed and appeared to be in a state of extreme distress. The collective gasp that escaped from the lips of the onlookers echoed through the cavern, their senses reeling from the unexpected and appalling discovery.

As the chilling reality of the scene sank in, Palki Trivedi could only manage to whisper breathlessly, her voice trembling, "It seems as if these all are…" Before she could complete her sentence, Sophia, her voice equally hushed finished the thought, "Shards in the Sky….". With the macabre sight indelibly imprinted in their memories, they ventured deeper into the fortress.

As the team advanced further into the underground fortress, they stumbled upon a shocking sight; an injured and heavily wounded

Maxx Nickolav, the once-formidable figure who had orchestrated the syndicate's operations. Instinctively, they moved to offer assistance. However, as they approached to lend a helping hand, Maxx's actions took them by surprise.

In a sudden and desperate manoeuvre, he produced a pistol from his concealed position and unleashed a scream that reverberated through the cavern "Da zdravstvuyet Koroleva Nikolave!" (Long Live, Queen Nickolav!) And he shot himself dead. The war had ended. The entire syndicate had been eliminated save the Queenpin, Queen Nickolav.

The KOBRA commandos and the SWAT team had sacrificed their own. The toll was heavy. Among the fallen heroes was Mr. Kaur, the valiant leader of the SWAT team. His loss was deeply felt by all, for he had demonstrated unwavering courage and leadership throughout the mission. Mr. Kaur's sacrifice would forever be remembered. The team stood in silence and mourned the dead.

With the offensive operation against the syndicate's fortress concluded, a new and equally critical phase was about to begin: the rescue operation for the hundreds of captive girls and women hanging in the cages beneath the blue ceiling. Palki Trivedi, recognizing the enormity of the task ahead immediately set her formidable organizational skills into motion.

Palki knew that the rescue operation required massive manpower and resources. Without hesitation, she began reaching out to various organizations and agencies. Phone calls were made to news channels, local and international NGOs, and the fire department.The rescue operation was a complex endeavour with the girls belonging to different nationalities.

Palki orchestrated a coordinated effort, involving not only local authorities but also embassies and consulates from around the world. It was an international crisis that demanded a unified response. Recognizing the trauma that the rescued girls would undoubtedly be experiencing, Palki also arranged for counselling centres to be on standby.

Trained professionals would provide immediate support to help the survivors cope with the physical and emotional scars of their captivity. The logistics of providing shelter, medical care, and basic necessities for the rescued girls were also addressed. Temporary facilities were set up to ensure their well-being and safety during the transition to a new life.

News channels not only reported the rescue operation but also mobilized support from around the world. The global community was alerted to the plight of these girls, prompting an outpouring of assistance and solidarity. The rescue operation became a multinational effort. Agencies and organizations from across the world pooled their resources and expertise.

It was a testament to the power of international cooperation in the face of a humanitarian crisis.As the rescue operation got underway, the team knew that their mission was far from over. Saving the Shards in the Sky was a monumental task, one that would require unwavering dedication,resources, and the support of the global community.

Together, they had brought an end to the nightmare that had ensnared these innocent lives and offered them a chance at a brighter and safer future.

Chapter 11

The Aftermath!

In the aftermath of their daring and successful mission, ACP Wagle called for a debriefing at Mount Erebus; a moment to reflect on their achievements, acknowledge their sacrifices, and plan for the challenges that lay ahead. With a sense of pride and gratitude, ACP Wagle addressed the assembly, "Congratulations to each and every one of you.

Our success today is a testament to your unwavering dedication, bravery, and exceptional teamwork." He continued, "I want to extend my deepest appreciation to the Sisterhood, Simmy, Rocko, Mr. Ranavde, Mr. Ramanna. And, with the utmost respect, to the late Mr. Kaur, who made the ultimate sacrifice in the line of duty. His memory will forever be etched in our hearts.

"And last but certainly not least," ACP Wagle concluded, "A special commendation goes to Palki Trivedi". The round of applause that followed ACP Wagle's heartfelt words echoed through the room, a collective expression of gratitude and solidarity among the team. ACP Wagle gestured for Palki Trivedi to share the good news that was yet to be revealed.

She began, "Thank you all for your kind words and support. While our mission was undoubtedly challenging, there's another piece of news that I'm delighted to share with you all." She continued, "Amidst our operations, we received word from authorities that the syndicate's network is crumbling". Everyone was thrilled to hear this piece of news.

"Thanks to the evidence we've gathered and the dismantling of key operations, the authorities are making significant progress in apprehending those responsible for these heinous crimes." This was followed by a loud round of applause.

Palki Trivedi's announcement electrified the room. The prospect of her taking on the position of Chief of the International Anti-Trafficking Department was met with a tremendous outpouring of joy and excitement. As the applause swelled, it was accompanied by enthusiastic whistling and cheers, creating a euphoric atmosphere that resonated with pride and support.

Palki continued, "While we have achieved significant victories and dismantled key elements of the syndicate, we must acknowledge that the most formidable adversary, Queen Nickolav, remains shrouded in mystery. It appears she has gone into hiding. We've no concrete leads or information about her whereabouts. Rest assured, we will tirelessly pursue her until she is apprehended."

"There is more news I want to share. Amelia, Elena, Isabella, Olivia and Sophia's names have been put forward for the prestigious President's Bravery Award". A resounding cheer erupted in honour of the Sisterhood. Mr. Kaur will posthumously receive a gallantry award from the President". The room lapsed into silence at the mention of his name.

The memory of his bravery and sacrifice brought tears to the eyes of everyone present. Even in the stern visage of ACP Wagle, there were subtle hints of teardrops welling up. A two-minute silence was observed in honour of Mr. Kaur. "We depart for now," ACP Wagle spoke with a hint of both nostalgia and anticipation, "but we will meet again for another adventure."

The Sisterhood were to be felicitated with the President's Bravery Award on Republic Day Parade watched by millions of people in India and across the world. The story of the Sisterhood's collective efforts and determination in crushing the trafficking syndicate quickly became a national headline capturing the hearts and imaginations of people across the country.

News of the Sisterhood's success in dismantling the trafficking syndicate was prominently featured in newspapers, news channels, and online media. Their story resonated deeply with the public, serving as a source of inspiration and hope in the fight against such heinous crimes. The recognition and honour bestowed upon the Sisterhood didn't stop at the President's Bravery Award.

They were also set to receive special commendations and medals from the Honourble Chief Minister of Maharashtra, Mr. Eknath Shinde. Meeting him was a moment of immense honour and pride for Amelia, Elena, Isabella, Olivia, and Sophia. As they stood before him, they received their commendations and medals personally from the esteemed leader of the state.

The invitation from the Honourable Chief Minister of Kerala, Mr. Pinarayi Vijayan was a special event to acknowledge their remarkable efforts. Mr. Vijayan's recognition of their exceptional efforts swelled their hearts with a deep sense of pride. During the event, he engaged in a conversation with them, spoke before the press, and lauded their unwavering commitment and heroism.

Receiving a special invitation from the Honourable Prime Minister of India, Mr. Narendra Modi was an extraordinary honour for the Sisterhood. Being acknowledged by the Prime Minister was an affirmation of their impact on society and a validation of their unwavering commitment to justice. During the press meet that followed, Mr. Modi's words resonated deeply with everyone.

He not only commended the Sisterhood for their exceptional bravery but also used the opportunity to address the young girls of India. His advice, encouraging them to be inspired by the Sisterhood and to be strong and brave like them struck a powerful chord. Tears welled up in their eyes as they realized the far-reaching impact of their actions.

They were not only being recognized but also being held up as role models for the young girls of India, an honour that carried great responsibility and meaning. They knew that they had become symbols of hope and empowerment for the next generation, inspiring countless young girls to stand up for justice and pursue their dreams with courage and determination.

The Sisterhood gathered at the opulent Taj for a joyous occasion; the wedding of Erica and John. It was a day filled with love, happiness, and celebration that brought both families together in sheer delight. The two families embraced each other; their hearts filled with joy as they left the troubles of the past behind. Their happiness was not just for themselves but also for John and Erica.

The wedding took place in a magnificent ballroom at the Taj, adorned with grand chandeliers, rich drapery, and opulent floral arrangements. The room exuded elegance, with floor-to-ceiling windows offering breath-taking views of the city skyline. The ballroom exuded an enchanting ambiance, where romance blossomed in every corner.

Elena wore a stunning dress in a complementary shade to Erica's ivory gown. Her dress featured an elegant A-line silhouette, with delicate lace detailing that added a touch of sophistication. The dress had a subtle, off-the-shoulder neckline and a flowing train that trailed behind her gracefully. She completed her look with exquisite pearl-encrusted shoes and a set of heirloom diamond jewellery.

Sophia wore a classic, floor-length gown with a sweetheart neckline and intricate beadwork that shimmered in the soft lighting. The dress was in a deep shade of midnight blue, perfectly contrasting with the ivory and pastel colour scheme of the wedding. Sophia's ensemble was complemented by elegant silver stilettos and a vintage sapphire necklace.

Olivia opted for a more contemporary and chicer look. Her dress was a sleek and form-fitting, off-the-shoulder design. The gown was adorned with minimalist beading, adding a touch of modern glamour to her ensemble. Olivia completed her modern and chic look with strappy silver sandals and a statement sapphire bracelet that beautifully accentuated her style.

Isabella's dress was a dreamy pastel hue that matched the wedding's colour palette. Her gown had a romantic, flowing skirt with layers of tulle and a bodice adorned with delicate floral appliqués. It was a perfect blend of whimsy and elegance. Isabella's look was elevated with dainty ballet flats and a pearl-embellished headband.

Amelia wore a floor-length gown with a high neckline and a subtle mermaid silhouette. The dress was accented with intricate lace patterns that extended down to a dramatic train, creating an aura of timeless elegance. Amelia's elegant look was completed with vintage-inspired satin pumps and a vintage heirloom pearl necklace.

Erica's wedding dress was a classic A-line gown, crafted from the finest ivory silk satin. The dress featured a fitted bodice with a sweetheart neckline that delicately framed her collarbones, enhancing her graceful neck and shoulders. The bodice was adorned with intricate lace appliqués that cascaded down the length of the gown, creating a sense of romance and ethereal beauty.

The skirt of the gown flowed gracefully to the floor, pooling into a dramatic train that trailed behind her as she walked. The train was embellished with delicate lace motifs that added a touch of sophistication to the ensemble. Erica's dress was both timeless and elegant, evoking a sense of regal charm. Erica chose to keep her jewellery simple and understated.

She desired the focus to remain on her gown and her natural beauty. She wore a delicate pearl necklace and matching pearl earrings, adding a touch of classic elegance to her bridal look. The pearls shimmered softly in the light, complementing her gown's ivory hue. Erica's wedding shoes were a perfect blend of style and comfort.

She opted for ivory satin heels with a moderate heel height, ensuring she could move gracefully throughout the day without sacrificing style. The shoes were adorned with subtle crystal embellishments, adding a hint of sparkle to her ensemble. Erica's beauty transcended boundaries and realms. She resembled a beautiful nymph from the celestial realms.

John wore a classic black tuxedo. The jacket was single-breasted with satin peak lapels adding a touch of luxury and classic refinement to his look. The trousers were perfectly tailored to his frame, completing the sleek silhouette. Underneath his tuxedo jacket, John wore a crisp white dress shirt with a classic spread collar and French cuffs.

To complete his look, John added a white pocket square neatly folded into his jacket's breast pocket, providing a subtle contrast against the black ensemble. He also wore classic black patent leather shoes, polished to a high shine, and black dress socks. As a final touch, John wore a simple yet elegant white rose boutonniere on his lapel.

The decorations were a symphony of colours and textures. The colour scheme of soft pastels, gold accents, and fresh flowers graced every corner of the venue. Fairy lights twinkled overhead, adding a touch of magic to the evening. The ambiance was filled with melodious tunes as a live band serenaded the guests with soulful love ballads during dinner to upbeat melodies for dancing.

The music created an enchanting atmosphere that celebrated the couple's union. Following the exchange of vows, the newlyweds moved gracefully to the centrepiece of the reception; the wedding cake. The cake was a masterpiece of culinary artistry, a towering confection that stood as a symbol of their union and shared commitment.

The wedding cake was a multi-tiered masterpiece, adorned with intricate white fondant and delicate sugar flowers that matched the floral motifs seen throughout the wedding decor. Each layer of the cake was a different flavour, ensuring that there was something to delight every guest's palate. The top tier featured a figurine of a bride and groom.

It was a sweet and sentimental touch that added to the cake's charm. With a gentle smile and a shared moment of anticipation, John and Erica picked up the cake-cutting knife together, their hands intertwined. The room fell silent in anticipation as they made the first cut into the cake, a tradition that marked the beginning of their life together as husband and wife.

As they fed each other the first slice of cake, the guests erupted into joyous applause and cheers. With their vows exchanged, cake cut, and the formalities of the wedding ceremony complete, it was time for the celebration to truly begin. The guests eagerly awaited the music and dance that would set the stage for a night of joyful festivities.

The DJ and a live band took their place ready to serenade the newlyweds and their guests with a harmonious blend of melodies. The dance floor beckoned. And as the first notes of music filled the room, couples and friends made their way to the centre, ready to let loose and revel in the joyous atmosphere. The dance floor quickly became the focal point of the celebration.

Guests of all ages joined in, moving to the rhythm of the music. Laughter and smiles were abundant. Friends and family danced celebrating the love and happiness that John and Erica's union brought to their lives. The music played on, a mix of romantic ballads for slow dances and lively tunes that invited everyone to let go and enjoy the festivities.

It was a night of dancing, laughter, and celebration; a fitting way to mark the beginning of John and Erica's life together as a married couple. As the lively round of dancing continued, Sophia's phone suddenly rang, breaking the rhythm of the music. She glanced at her phone. Her brows furrowed in curiosity when she saw that it was an unknown number calling.

The Sisterhood, sensing something unusual, decided to move away from the deafening din of the music.In a hushed corner of the room, Sophia answered the call.

Sophia: *Da zdravstvuyet Sestrichestvo!*

Long live the Sisterhood!

As Sophia answered the call in Russian, there was a stunned silence on the other end. A thunderous guffaw erupted and a voice boomed.

Queen Nickolav:*My skoro vstretimsya!*

We will meet soon.

Bud't egotovy k Adskomu ognyu!

Get ready for Hellfire!

Sophia: *Sestrichestvo budet zhdat'.*

The Sisterhood will be waiting!

With a collective wave of excitement coursing through their veins, they made their way back to the dance floor. As the first beats of a lively tune filled the air, they shouted in chorus, "Long Live the Sisterhood!" With the music guiding their every move, they began to dance with wild abandon, a whirlwind of energy and joy. As they danced into the night, their spirits soared.

The memory of the mysterious phone call only added to the sense of adventure and camaraderie that defined their unique bond. The Sisterhood was alive and well, ready to face whatever challenges and mysteries lay ahead, one dance step at a time.

□

9 789359 737263